Western Civilization in World History

This engaging, informed, and astute book...is at once both lively overview and measured commentary. Providing a usable framework for thinking about western civilization, the work simultaneously and zestfully covers the high points in its historiography. It is truly a masterwork because of its versatility and the erudition on which it draws.

Bonnie Smith, Rutgers University

Western civilization and world history are often seen as different, or even mutually exclusive, routes into historical studies. This volume shows that they can be successfully linked, providing a tool to see each subject in the context of the other, identifying influences and connections.

Western Civilization in World History takes up the recent debates about the merits of the well-established "Western civ" approach versus the newer field of world history. Peter N. Stearns outlines key aspects of Western civilization – often assumed rather than analyzed – and reviews them in a global context.

Subjects covered include:

- how did the tradition of teaching "Western civ" evolve?
- when did Western civilization begin and what areas does it span?
- what distinguishes the West from the rest of the world?
- what is the place of Western civilization in today's globalized world?

This is an essential guide for students and teachers of both Western civilization and world history, which points to a more integrated, comparative way of studying history.

Peter N. Stearns is Provost and Professor of History at George Mason University. He has taught Western civilization and world history for decades and has published widely on both, including *The Other Side of Western Civilization* (5th edn, 1999) and *Experiencing World History* (2000). He currently chairs the Advanced Placement V

Themes in World History
Series editor: Peter N. Stearns

The *Themes in World History* series offers focused treatment of a range of human experiences and institutions in the world history context. The purpose is to provide serious, if brief, discussions of important topics as additions to textbook coverage and document collections. The treatments will allow students to probe particular facets of the human story in greater depth than textbook coverage allows, and to gain a fuller sense of historians' analytical methods and debates in the process. Each topic is handled over time – allowing discussions of change and continuities. Each topic is assessed in terms of a range of different societies and religions – allowing comparisons of relevant similarities and differences. Each book in the series helps readers deal with world history in action, evaluating global contexts as they work through some of the key components of human society and human life.

Gender in World History
Peter N. Stearns

Consumerism in World History
Peter N. Stearns

Warfare in World History
Michael S. Neiberg

Disease and Medicine in World History
Sheldon Watts

Asian Democracy in World History
Alan T. Wood

Western Civilization in World History

Peter N. Stearns

Routledge
Taylor & Francis Group

NEW YORK AND LONDON

First published 2003
by Routledge
29 West 35th Street, New York, NY 10001

Simultaneously published in the UK
by Routledge
11 New Fetter Lane, London EC4P 4EE

Routledge is an imprint of the Taylor & Francis Group

Typeset in Garamond and Gill by
Steven Gardiner Ltd, Cambridge
Printed and bound in Great Britain by
MPG Books Ltd, Bodmin, Cornwall

Library of Congress Cataloging in Publication Data
Stearns, Peter N.
Western civilization in world history / Peter N. Stearns
   p. cm.
Includes bibliographical references and index.
1. Civilization, Western – History. 2. World history. I. Title.
CB245.S743 2003
909'.09821 – dc21   2003002168

British Library Cataloguing in Publication Data
A catalogue record for this book is available from the British
Library

ISBN 0–415–31611–1 (hbk)
ISBN 0–415–31610–3 (pbk)

Contents

Acknowledgments

A vast number of people contributed to this book, beginning with my father, also a historian, and continuing through an array of gifted teachers and colleagues. Particular thanks, to Veronica Fletcher, who provided research assistance, Lawrence Beaber and Despina Danos, who contributed additional information. Kaparah Simmons helped me with the manuscript. My thanks also to Routledge and the series editor, Vicky Peters, for their guidance and support.

Chapter 1

Introduction

Why Western civ?

This is a book about Western civilization and how to fit it into thinking about world history. During the past 15 years American educators, and sometimes the general public, have been treated to vigorous debates about the merits of teaching Western civ versus those involved in the newer subject of world history. The debates continue today, as we will briefly detail below. Typically, they proceed in an either–or fashion: one must either be devoted to the special virtues of Western civilization or one must embrace the world history vision, and there is not much in between. Correspondingly, we lack materials that would help students in a Western civ class think about a world history framework, or those in world history to spend just a moment on issues specific to Western civ. This book seeks to provide this kind of intermediary, by suggesting the kind of analysis essential to thinking about Western civilization in a world history context.

I do not pretend to believe that the book will end debate. There is no question that choices have to be made between Western civilization and world history courses, in terms of the amount and nature of factual coverage and key aspects of the interpretive approach as well. Those who think that Western civ is a special experience that must be protected from the baleful influences of other civilizations will never be pleased by an effort to combine. And some world historians who see their mission as downplaying and attacking the West may not be conciliated either, though this is frankly a lesser problem because the passions are not as widely shared, at least in the United States.

Still, this essay does proceed on the premise that we can do better in linking the two subjects than we have in the past. And there is a second premise: one of the problems in talking about Western civ, whether in world history context or more generally, is that several crucial issues in presenting Western civilization have not been well articulated. More has been assumed about Western civ than has been analyzed, and this book, though briefly, brashly takes up this challenge as well.

This chapter deals primarily with the current educational debate – what the fuss is all about, and why such intense emotions are involved on both sides. We then turn, in Chapter 2, to a brief history of the Western civ course itself, for a century now a staple in much college and some high school education in the United States. This allows a fuller sense of how and why people became so attached to the Western civ tradition, but also why some of the key issues surrounding Western civ as a subject were often ignored. Subsequent chapters then turn to the interpretation of Western civilization itself, in a world history context – not to present a lot of textbook facts, which are readily available in Western civ surveys and even many world history textbooks – but to highlight what needs to be thought about, and argued about, in dealing with Western civilization as a historical subject.

First, the recent furor. In the fall of 1994, a commission of historians, nationally recruited as part of a multi-discipline effort to define secondary school standards, issued a thick book defining goals in world history. This followed on the heels of another volume, on US history standards. Both efforts drew a storm of protest. Predictably, US history served as lightning rod, with hosts of objections to heroes left out, less familiar features emphasized. But world history drew its brickbats too, from a variety of conservative commentators who thought the world approach detracted from the special emphasis needed on Western achievements and landmarks. With some justification, the World Standards were seen as not only insufficiently Western, but too prone to define other civilization traditions neutrally or even positively while critically probing Western deficiencies such as racism and leadership in the early modern slave trade. In a daunting 99–1 vote, the US Senate denounced the Standards effort. While the vote focused mainly on US history, the Senate ventured its larger world view in stipulating that any recipients of federal money "should have a decent respect for the contributions of Western civilization." The resolution had no legal force but, as one observer noted, the effect on history education was potentially "chilling."

This was not the end of story, as we will discuss later on. Further, it occurred at the crest of conservative congressional insurgency, with Congressman Newt Gingrich's Contract with America movement riding into town just a few days after the ill-timed Standards hit the streets. But it demonstrated the tremendous gap between what a number of history educators thought was important, outside the US history realm, and what key segments of the wider public seemed to value.

And debate has continued. Many states, after the National Standards project foundered, introduced their own history and social studies criteria. While many of these used a "world history" rubric, the facts and values they thought students should learn were predominantly Western. Conservative regents or trustees at many universities saw, as part of their mission, a need to insist on a required Western civ course as part of a general education program. In one case I was personally involved in, a partisan Board forced a Western civ requirement down the throats of a reluctant faculty (which had, however, been willing to install a looser Western and American values and institutions rubric). The initial proposal not only insisted on a single course, but argued that it should end in 1815 – presumably because after that point Western civilization went downhill with developments such as socialism and modern art, though I confess I never understood exactly what was intended. Happily this particular constraint was lifted, but the requirement remained. Members of the Board felt passionately that exposure to Western civ was a central part of proper education, even at the cost of public controversy and a nasty if short-lived dispute with the faculty. And there were others, educators as well as political partisans, who saw a new mission in maintaining or reviving Western civ courses in the 1990s and 2000s, as an essential criterion for the educated person.

Even the tragedy of 9.11.2001 brought controversy. Most Americans reacted to the terrorist attack with the realization that we needed to know more about the world as a whole, and particularly about Islam and central Asia. But a conservative counterthrust, sparked in part by Lynn Cheney, the wife of the nation's Vice President, argued that the nature of the attack showed how essential it was to rally around Western standards, which in turn must not be diluted by curricula that focused diffusely on the world as a whole.

West versus world has, for almost two decades, been enmeshed in what some have aptly called the "culture wars" in the United States. One group, the cosmopolitans, have argued that since we live in and are affected by the world as a whole, we need to know about it, that a narrow focus on the West alone does not provide the breadth of understanding required in an age of globalization. Some members of the group also worry about the limitations of certain Western values, and even see a world history approach as a means of West-bashing. And while this is not the most common approach in the world history camp, it is often argued that a world perspective will help students gain the capacity to step outside their own value system to take a critical, though not necessarily hostile, look at potential limitations and parochialisms. The other group, more conservative, sees such special values in Western civ that its centrality must be maintained. Their insistence reflects a sincere, though debatable, sense that the West is a distinctively rich civilization tradition, from which among other things basic American values flow. But there are extraneous factors involved as well, beyond the nature of Western civ itself: a belief that globalization, or the deterioration of American youth, or the increasingly diverse racial and cultural origins of the American population (and particularly its young), or some combination of these issues, requires inculcation of Western civ as an antidote.

The clash of world views is fascinating, and not easily resolved. But it raises a number of key questions. First – and this one will preoccupy us recurrently throughout this essay: how much does the extra baggage thrown into the pleas for Western civ distort our historical understanding? If Western civ instruction is intended to discipline diverse cultures within the United States, for example, does this also involve a tendency to preach and whitewash, rather than analyze the Western experience? We will see that, as the tradition of teaching Western civ developed during the 20th century, so many matters were assumed that key questions – including, sometimes, a careful discussion of when Western civ began or even precisely where it was located – were left untouched. Many of these problems are fixable, but they must be addressed if Western civ teaching is to live up to its promise.

The second set of questions involves the possibility of reconciliation. There is no hope of bridging the gap between West-is-best conservatives and the West-bashing minority in the world history camp. They seek to argue about values, and use and distort history only as a pretext for their cultural campaigns. But lots of folks between the partisan extremes may sensibly wonder, why not do a bit of both. Indeed, many high school world history courses attempt to do precisely this, by calling themselves world history but spending two-thirds of their time dealing with the West. The problem is that this compromise does not do justice to global issues – for they are constantly seen through a Western lens – and sometimes fails really to analyze the West as well. Students are left with a pile of facts about the West, and scattered forays into other regions, with little but mishmash as result. But other compromises can be imagined. Students could take their Western course in high school, and then a world survey in college – if conservatives would relax their relentless pretensions to define purity in college-level general education. Even here, there are drawbacks: what about the students who do not go on to college but who nevertheless need some perspective on the wider world? What about the many students who do not remember high school work well enough to integrate it with college instruction?

Clearly, American education would benefit from some explicit experiments in combining Western and world history through various kinds of sequencing – experiments that are difficult, however, in the current culture wars climate. But even before experimentation, we can begin to improve on the existing roadblock by thinking about Western civ differently – actively, but differently, in ways that can better help relate it to world history. Through this, in turn, we can reduce the needless either-or qualities of the West versus world curricular quagmire. This is the goal this book seeks to serve.

A brief personal note, and then some concluding points for this intro-duction. I was trained in European history, and my first teaching job was devoted to teaching Western civ (at the University of Chicago, where the Western civ tradition remains particularly strong). I loved the Western civ survey I took as a college freshmen. The fascination of European history, and the enthusiasm of several of the instructors, really drew me into the history field. In retrospect, I can also see that the course bypassed some of the questions it should have explored concerning Western civ, but I was not aware of the limitations at the time. And, even in believing now that a Western civ diet by itself is too restrictive, I continue to honor the values of a good Western civ course and the devotion of many of those who teach it. I also enjoyed many aspects of my University of Chicago experience, though by then I was beginning to question some of the Western civ assumptions that particular course involved. Particularly, I was concerned about assuming that great philosophical ideas and Western civilization were the same thing. I worried a bit, also, about the exclusion of the rest of the world – intriguingly, one of the first great American world historians, William McNeill, was teaching at Chicago at precisely this time, though he could not dent the Western civ commitment at his own institution. And I really wondered about the purist insistence, in the Chicago course at that time, that the Western civ course should end around 1900 because the 20th century was such a dreadful distortion of true Western values; that was and is not my view of the responsibilities of good history teaching, which involves helping students connect present and past and dealing with problems as well as glories, and I joined some other recent hires in getting this revealing aspect of the course changed.

Some years later I was converted to world history, mainly on the simple grounds that we live in the world, not the West alone, and we need a commensurate historical perspective. I also came to find the interpretive issues involved in thinking about world history intriguing, and realized that the field was manageable – ambitious, but not impossibly vast. I have participated and will continue to participate in efforts to move college and school curricula away from Western civ alone, and toward a world history approach. I have worked with many teachers making the transition from Western civ training to a world history course. Not surprisingly, some find the need to develop new materials and new conceptual categories difficult; routines can be comforting. But many find the newer perspectives exciting, and even realize that their understanding of the West itself can improve in the process.

In a sense this essay is an attempt to combine a past love, richly rewarding at the time, with a newer commitment in which I deeply believe. By thinking about Western civ differently, with the world history context front and center, some of us can have a bit of our cake and eat it too.

For in the long run, world history will win – various forms of it, to be sure, not a single version. The reasons for it are simply too compelling: in a nation obviously affected by religious schooling in Pakistan, or state support of banks in Japan, or disease patterns in Africa, or cooking from Mexico, the need to gain a global perspective is inescapable. In the long run again – how long, I confess I do not know – the rearguard defense of Western civ will seem an anachronism, a desperate attempt to avoid acknowledging the multicultural nature of American society and the larger impact of the world we live in. For as a colleague recently noted, quite simply, the rest of the world is most of the world. We cannot ignore it educationally or in any other way.

But attention to Western civ need not disappear in the process. If we begin to think of Western civ through a new lens, asking the questions about it that need to be answered from a world history standpoint, we can improve the inevitable result and invite more imaginative integrations along the way.

We can start by two adjustments. The first, terribly difficult for people steeped in Western history including many teachers, involves pruning the facts. All history is selective; even huge Western civ texts leave out more than they include. But in order to think about Western history flexibly, in ways compatible with world history, we need a willingness to leave out or truncate some familiar staples. This essay, of course, does not pretend to provide all the facts an appropriate treatment of Western civ may warrant, but it does suggest particular highlights and key issues, around which a longer but still streamlined version can be developed.

The second adjustment involves thinking about Western civ not as *the* civilization (even if you still believe it is *our* civilization), but as one of several – and neither the oldest nor the easiest to define. Like all major civilizations, it offers a mix of strengths and weaknesses. Like all, it has experienced, and will experience, ups and downs, not a straight trajectory toward ever-greater importance. Like all, it can be fully grasped, not by endless exploration of its details, but by comparison and by juxtaposition to larger world processes.

One final point. This is a short book, on really big issues. It is meant to provoke thought and discussion, even disagreement, not to provide final words on complex subjects. Indeed, some sections are really more questions than answers, as we seek to explore some new ways of thinking about an old subject.

And again, our effort will come in two stages: first, the brief history of Western civ as a teaching field, which will help us understand some common assumptions and confusions and in the process explore why many people are so excited about the Western civ course as a symbol of good education. Second, an interpretation of the Western experience itself in comparative and global context.

According to tradition, when the Indian nationalist leader Gandhi was once asked what he thought about Western civilization, he presumably replied that he thought it would be a very good idea. The fact that the word "civilization" has several meanings – something world historians have worried about a lot, but those in the Western civ tradition somewhat less so – is one of the issues we have to grapple with.

Further reading

Lynn Cheney, *Telling the Truth: Why Our Culture and Our Country Have Stopped Making Sense and What We Can Do About It* (New York: Simon & Schuster, 1995); Gary Nash and Ross Dunn, *History on Trial: Cultural Wars and the Teaching of the Past* (New York: A. A. Knopf: Distributed by Random House, 1997).

Part 1

The Western civ tradition

Most studies of Western civilization begin with the history of the civilization, not the history of how the civilization has been taught. In this case, however, a brief exploration of how Western civ programs emerged, what problems they were intended to solve, is essential as a backdrop to the exploration of the subject itself. Too often a subject like Western civ (or American literature, or calculus) is taken as a given by students and teachers alike. In fact, it is always legitimate to identify and test basic assumptions, and the history of the teaching program offers a way to do so. Then we can turn to the analysis of how the assumptions play out in the subject matter itself.

Chapter 2

Why Western civ courses
The constraints of success

It may seem surprising that formal Western civ courses are both relatively recent (only introduced in the early 20th century) and American. Both points can be explained, in the process revealing some of the strengths and limitations of the Western civ approach.

It is also important to note, as a subset of the second point, how unusual it is for a nation to become so strongly committed to a history not directly its own. By the late 19th century, most countries were busily organizing historical training into national categories, in order to instill patriotism. This occurred in the United States, and in some instances the emphasis on American history preempted Western civ (largely the case in Texas, for example). But for many educators, and in their wake some segments of the public, American history by itself seemed too narrow, too purely recent, and so the commitment to Western civ, though technically foreign, developed as a complement. This point, too, can be explored, and, of course, it is vital to understand why American conservatives today, so strongly nationalist in most respects, place such weight on the Western civ tradition.

There are several precedents to the Western civ course. As Christianity developed, both in Western and Eastern Europe, various monks wrote chronicles of Christendom. These were usually descriptive, what happened one year after the next, and the selection of data was somewhat random. They did assume, however, that Christendom was a unifying concept to frame historical accounts. This picture was muddied, of course, by divisions between Catholic and orthodox Christianity. Russian chronicles talked of Russia, perhaps parts of the Balkans, and the Byzantine Empire, while French or German monks focused on the territory administered by the Roman church. But the idea of some coherence, transcending narrow and changing political boundaries, was nevertheless important.

The idea of history developed in the Italian Renaissance, from the 14th century onward, and then spread to the north, offered a much more direct precedent. A key development here was the sense that the Greek and Roman past constituted an immense treasure trove for modern intellectuals and educators. Not only philosophical ideas and artistic styles, but also historical examples could and should be directly borrowed. From this, the belief emerged that any member of the educated elite should be trained in Latin, possibly in Greek, and certainly in important segments of classical history. Knowing what Roman generals and politicians had done was directly relevant to policy issues and character development in the Renaissance world. Of course, most people in the Western world did not have access to this kind of education, so exposure to classical history and the ability to cite events and biographies from the Athenian or Roman republics became an important badge of elite social status as well.

The current Western civ teaching tradition altered both of these precedents to a degree. It certainly assumed that Western civilization could not be captured exclusively by attention to Christianity, though religion had to be considered. It also assumed that the Western past involved more than Greece and Rome, and that knowledge of its unfolding was essential to the education and citizenship of numbers of people, and not just a narrow elite. But the Western civ tradition was built on its precedents also: it did sometimes drift into a chronicling of events in the West, on the assumption that they would speak for themselves. It did sometimes pay particular deference to Greece and Rome, without much explicit analysis concerning why this was due. And it did continue to harbor some elitist impulses. It is not entirely accidental that, even today, many of the staunchest defenders of the Western civ course sit in some of the Ivy League colleges and in wannabe liberal arts institutions that sincerely believe they are training the best and the brightest and providing them, through Western civ, with a means of distinguishing themselves.

One other component contributed to the emergence of Western civ. Formal, professional historical teaching and research emerged in the second half of the 19th century. Obviously, as we have already suggested, history writing was not new at all. But the notion that there are professional standards for historical work, and that some people could and should be formally trained in its practice, for example through receiving doctoral degrees in the subject, arose in the later 19th century. The center for the development was in Europe, particularly Germany; some credit the German historian Leopold von Ranke, with his commitment to portraying history "as it actually happened", as the first professional historical researcher. The European origins of this development meant that many of the early American professionals were trained in Europe or by Europeans, so they naturally assumed that European historical topics were appropriate fodder for research and teaching alike. This helps explain why, at a place like the Kansas State University (then called Kansas State Agricultural College) around 1900, along with some courses in American history, the standard curriculum included offerings in British history (seen as a particularly important backdrop to the United States), ancient, medieval, modern European, and also French history. As the 1909 catalogue indicated: "in order really to understand American history you must know European history. This is one of the chief reasons . . .

for our study of ancient and modern history." Indeed, in American universities generally in 1910, 45% of all history courses dealt with Western Europe, along with another 16% on England, compared to 37% on the United States, (and, obviously, 2% on the rest of the world).

Even with this pattern, however, the Western civ course had not quite yet emerged. Scientific historical researchers in Europe, and most of their American trainees, tended to focus on detailed research on relatively small periods of time. They were not comfortable with grand sweeps of a civilization; and so the European history courses tended to be subdivided into discrete time periods such as ancient or medieval. Putting together a larger picture, if done at all, would be mainly done by the student. Furthermore, the rise of professional history occurred at a time of growing nationalism. This meant that much research, and even more teaching, tended to be divided into national categories, often designed to bolster the claims of the nation state. Particularly for the modern period, history programs in Europe itself were thus typically focused on one's own nation, not a larger civilization. And nationalist historians even quarreled about earlier times, before nations existed: Germans around 1900 tended to argue that the Middle Ages owed most to the proud traditions of Germanic tribes, and less to the achievements of the Roman empire, while the French, taking up the Latin mantle, argued the reverse. It was not easy, amid this kind of contention, to think of larger wholes; hence, at Kansas State, courses were on England or France rather than a whole civilization from beginning to present.

Two developments, coalescing in the first quarter of the 20th century in the United States, amended this context in ways that generated the tradition of the Western civ course in many American colleges and universities, from the 1920s onward. They help explain, also, why the Western civ impulse took hold in the United States more than in Western Europe itself. One of the developments was personal, in the contributions of a singularly imaginative and persistent history teacher. The other development, more complex, involved curricular reactions to some troubling changes in the world of the early 20th century.

The first force highlighted an individual, James Harvey Robinson, who taught both undergraduate and graduate students at Columbia University and who tirelessly produced both textbooks and readings collections to serve as the basis for the teaching of Western civ. Robinson preached what he called the "new history," which in turn involved an emphasis on relatively long spans of time. Advances in evolutionary biology and in archeology had placed new emphasis on extensive units of time and permitted a new division between human "prehistory" (which mainly meant, before writing) and "history." Historical time was relatively recent – though far longer than smaller chunks like "medieval" – and through it, current developments could easily be connected to the historical past. With this kind of thinking it also seemed logical to distinguish between peoples with a history, such as those in the

West, and peoples – such as many of those in Africa – whose long lack of writing seemed to deprive them of this quality. This distinction is now almost entirely discredited as we will see, but in the hands of people like Robinson it helped situate Western history in a special place. While the idea of prehistory had first emerged in 1871, as an English language term, it was Robinson, who was a professor at Columbia from 1895 to 1919, who most clearly translated the notion into a basis for a transnational history survey course.

It was probably inevitable, given the Christian, Renaissance and professional history precedents, that Robinson would see his historical story in European terms. There was a single survey, from the origins of historical time to the present, and it centered in Europe with recent extensions to North America. This was "our" history, and it united ancient Greece and thinkers like Aristotle with modern Europe and Newton and Darwin. Robinson talked easily of a "unity and continuity in history" in ways that had not seemed obvious to some of his predecessors. Indeed, it was both a measure of Robinson's achievement, and a real fault, that many teachers stopped thinking about unity and continuity as problems, and converted them to assumptions.

Two other points: Robinson's vision centered the essence of history on intellectual rather than political achievements. This was vital for the emergence of a Western civ course – for, whatever its merits, the Western past has not involved political unity, but it has arguably entailed some common intellectual contributions from various places within the West. And second, Robinson's sense of Western unity involved an emphasis on the rational and scientific and on a relatively steady line of progress. The present was connected to the Western past, it built on it, but it also improved it. And implicitly – here was another powerful assumption that was not hauled out for careful analysis – this Western quality of rationalism and progress contrasted it with the traditions of other regions even if, technically, they too had "histories." It was possible to distinguish Western history from the "other" without much explicit analysis, either because the other was mired in prehistorical conditions or because the other, though historical in the sense of having writing, was steeped in superstition and backwardness.

Between 1900 and 1915, Robinson constructed an extremely influential graduate course at Columbia that chronologically surveyed the rise of rational thought located in the West. By 1926, Western civ courses for undergraduates, patterned on this model, were becoming standard not only at Columbia, where the "Contemporary Civilization" course had been made a requirement in 1919, but more broadly, and a number of textbooks, quite similar to each other, emerged to service the field, unifying ancient, medieval and modern history into a single narrative that could be covered within a single academic year. Many of these texts were written by Robinson's former students, who had fanned out to other institutions, such as the University of Michigan, where they carefully replicated their mentor's approach. Harry

Elmer Barnes, in his 1930s text, repeated the standard assumptions: "The history of Western civilization cannot be confined within the older historical chronology. It is now realized that man has been on earth for at least a million years. . . . From the standpoint of time and culture alike, the whole civilization of man in the West since ancient Egyptian days is 'modern' in character." With this modern, Western unity so strongly stated, there was really no reason to go into any detail about the histories of other peoples, including those of what Barnes insisted on referring to as the "Orient," who clearly lagged behind the West.

But the rapid adoption and dissemination of the Western civ course required a special context, beyond the labors of Robinson and his trainees. Here is the second part of explaining "Why Western civ?" The new course built clearly on Renaissance ideas of the link between Greece and Rome and then-modern times. It owed much to social Darwinism – the kind of thinking that had followed on the discovery of evolutionary theory. Social Darwinism contributed more than the sense of a big sweep of time followed by the emergence of humans followed by the very recent emergence of civilization. It also encouraged distinctions among different races of people with very different potentials for evolutionary success. In the classic age of imperialism, it was not surprisingly assumed that Western peoples topped the evolutionary hierarchy, which made it easy to concentrate on their history and ignore that of other, inferior types whether literally prehistorical or not.

But there was more specific context still. World War I – which in its European origins and concentration was really a battle within the West – had drawn the United States closer to Europe but had also raised huge concerns about Europe's future. The greatest civilization in the world, which in the eyes of most American historians of Europe remained a vital compass for the United States itself, had split asunder. Many people on both sides of the Atlantic, though particularly in Europe itself, wondered if the West had passed its prime. The cruelties and losses in the War, the continuing postwar tensions and dislocations including a foreboding that more war might come, combined with stirrings in other parts of the world, such as China and Japan. American historians of Europe found a special mission in this situation, in providing a story of Western progress that rose above the nationalist limitations that bedeviled Europe itself. As Barnes put it, in writing his *Intellectual and Cultural History of the Western World*: "For the first time in human history, mankind is directly confronted with a compulsory and relatively expeditious choice between utopia and barbarism. . . . It is hoped that this book will contribute very directly to . . . [an] intelligent choice." Writing and teaching about Western civ became, for these authors, a way "to keep civilization alive."

The ironies here are obvious, and in some ways immensely appealing. Western civ courses sought to trace some durable features of a civilization, assumed to be the world's best, precisely because that civilization might be crumbling. The hope – and it could be fairly vague – was that emphasis on the historical positive might help prevent the contemporary negative, or, at the least, the United States itself might become a superior repository of Western values, even if the Old World persisted in going astray. The question of how to fit the inescapable evil in the Western world – the evil that for example created Nazism in the same decades that the Western civ course was taking root – was a complex problem. Some Western civ texts tried to address it. Others, such as the University of Chicago course that for a time simply left out the 20th century because it had turned so horrible, ducked. Again, the Western civ course was born of a number of very powerful assumptions that, precisely because they seemed so essential, were not tested very thoroughly.

And there was another, more strictly American part of the context – one that particularly explains the rapid spread of Western civ programs, often as required components of college and university general education programs.

High school education was becoming increasingly widespread in the first decades of the 20th century in the United States, particularly for the growing middle class. And an ever-increasing minority of high school graduates sought entry to college. Some aspired to the "best schools," headed by the Ivy League universities. It was difficult to turn all these students away – some were very able, some brought refreshing promise of representing expanding regions of the United States and present or future financial success. No longer did elite schools recruit simply from a handful of familiar private preparatory schools. But more diverse recruitment raised obvious problems of standards, for high schools varied greatly and their learning results might not be trustworthy. One response were College Board tests, introduced at this time to help identify aptitude regardless of school origin. Another response was a growing emphasis on general education requirements in college, that would help put students from different backgrounds on the same educational page. Required Western civ courses were often a key component in this process, doubly attractive since they harked back to older, Renaissance standards of elite education and because they purported to affirm the strength of Western values in troubling times.

But there was more. If Western civ spread in elite colleges, secondary schools might seek to imitate. Prep schools, anxious to affirm their superiority over rapidly expanding public high schools, tried to give their students a leg up on college entry by Western civ courses of their own. But many high schools could do the same. To be sure, at the public school level, Western civ courses almost always took a back seat to American history, which constituted the key and sometimes the only real history requirement. But they did spread widely.

And there was more still, at both school and college level. These same early 20th-century decades saw the rapid expansion of immigration into the United States, particularly from southern and eastern Europe. These were, by the racist Social Darwinist standards of the time, inferior peoples. There was some hope that they could be shunted off into special kinds of education, aimed narrowly at job training. Huge testing programs, designed to track students, aimed in this direction. But the fact was that the new immigrants were here to stay, and, however racist the climate, American authorities did not seek to deny them citizenship or education. So a new imperative emerged: Americanize them, as rapidly as possible.

In the history or social studies curriculum, the key response to this imperative was, of course, an upbeat, unifying American history course – or several, as students were often introduced to the same national facts and myths at many points from grade through high school. But Western civ could play a role here, too, precisely along the lines that Robinson and his heirs were indicating. American history, after all, however glorious, was pretty recent. A much more powerful image would emerge from a clear Western civ backdrop, that would show how American institutions and values were linked to the central, and appropriately glorious, traditions of Western civ in turn. Some of the new immigrants, such as the Italians, however inferior now, had played an earlier role in Western civilization, so their Americanization might be particularly hastened by appealing to common Western roots. Western civ became part, and sometimes a key part, of the response to a deeply felt need for explicit homogenization of the nation's diverse people, crucial for instilling a common sense of the past and a commitment to common values.

In some cases, the national and international purposes of Western civ could coalesce. Teaching about Western civilization was part of the War Aims educational program of the US army in World War I, designed in turn to teach American soldiers about the varied origins of the civilizational values they were fighting for. Or, by the 1930s or 1940s, a commitment to Western civ could allow for some special American pride. Western civ was still a story of progress, but the Europe of the 20th century was a mess. It was the United States that avoided fascism, that maintained a commitment to competitive capitalist values, that really embodied the best of the Western spirit. One way to handle the messier parts of the 20th century would be to wonder where the rest of the West went wrong, when the United States continued to show the true Western way.

Clearly, whatever the precise combination of factors involved, the commitment to Western civ not only involved an often unexamined set of intellectual assumptions, on the part of the Robinson group. It also involved a set of deeply-held but non-scholarly needs, which further reduced the likelihood that key assumptions would be subjected to much scrutiny. As Western civ responded to anxieties about the European motherland or about ethnic diversity and menace within the United States, it generated deep passions and commitments – but not necessarily a capacity for intelligent analysis.

European historians, certainly, were encouraged to sell their wares in terms of a civilizing mission. A University of Wisconsin medievalist, Dana Munro, thus argued that medieval history was essential as "preparation for a broad, enlightened citizenship. [The students] must have brought before them a point of view from which they can understand the civilization of their own times." Indeed, many university courses initially devised as studies in citizenship, inspired by the need to Americanize immigrants, soon converted to Western civ: this was true, for example, at both Stanford and Dartmouth.

For it was historians who largely captured the Western civ impulse, at least at the college level. This was not inevitable. And indeed there were movements by philosophers and literature departments to claim that their subjects could instill Western essentials too. Great books programs (like that at the University of Chicago) sometimes purported to convey the unities of the Western experience, and in some general education programs resultant courses did indeed complement the history survey. The idea of a Western literary canon, which educated students should be exposed to, continues to form part of conservative thinking about the Western civ curriculum. But the historians' appeal, derived from leaders such as Robinson, was ultimately more persuasive – in part, of course, because pure literature or philosophy could not connect as easily to problems of citizenship as could a history survey that included political as well as intellectual topics.

The results of this were great for European historians in the United States. There was far more market for one's expertise than would have otherwise existed. By the same token, of course, many history departments, and individual historians, became tied to the fate of Western civ programs, which could encourage a sense of routine-mindedness and a failure to tolerate criticism kindly. And even though Western civ programs in high schools were not as systematically developed (civics courses, among other things, taught citizenship directly, which reduced this argument for Western civ), many high school teachers, trained in the college Western civ tradition, continued to think of Western civ as the quintessential survey course, the source of truth and beauty in a history program. The later creation of an elite Advanced Placement program in European history to an extent built on, and perpetuated, this special reverence.

But the success of European historians in capturing the Western civ idea – initially, at least, for profoundly idealistic reasons – had one further effect, though some of this had been implicit in Robinson's own initial vision. Western civ courses often, though not always, became European history courses. That is, instead of focusing explicitly on a vision of what Western civilization consisted of, they turned to a presentation of an array of facts about the European experience. Not all of these facts were selected or questioned with the aims of Western civ in mind. Is it essential, for an understanding of the Western tradition, to know much about the Holy Roman Empire, or the Italian dispute between Guelphs and Ghibellines, or the English War of the Roses? Questions like this could be debated, but as Western civ texts increasingly became European history texts, they never even arose. And, of course, history testing is always most easily applied to specific chunks of factual knowledge, rather than analytical questions about what, if anything, was Western about this or that historical trend. So there tended to emerge (as in American history) an equation between factual competence in European history, based on textbooks that steadily expanded in size, and demonstrations of one's status as an educated person. And here, in a field already launched with some crucial unexamined assumptions, still other problems added in: many students, and indeed their teachers, were so busy covering and memorizing the facts that there was scant time not simply to analyze some of the key issues in the Western civ program, but to see that there were any analytical issues at all.

The growth of textbook size is really revealing. Initial Western civ texts ran from 400–700 pages (one of Robinson's efforts reached the high mark, but other treatments were much briefer). But as the Western civ course became enshrined, usually as a two-semester college history offering, the creep upward in factual detail began. By 2002 many Western civ texts were two volume productions, each tome around 900 pages, while a classic European-based *History of the Modern World* by R. R. Palmer and others had ballooned to over 1100 pages for the more recent centuries alone. Many texts were elegant productions, full of thoughtful judgments; but it was also possible that, amid the welter of detail, a concentration on the essentials of Western civ, however defined, might be obscured.

The origins and early evolution of the Western civ course show clearly why fervent passions were involved. A vision of history, deeply felt on the part of its creators, was joined with crucial concerns about the European world and the state of American citizenship in an age of immigration. People exposed to a Western civ course themselves might partake of this passion – even if they did not particularly like the course or remember it very well. A large subsection of professional historians in the United States became dependent on the program, whether they shared the passion or not – even though, as critics have pointed out, professional success consisted of escaping Western civ teaching as quickly as possible in favor of more specialized, upper-class or graduate courses.

The result, as Western civ became a general education staple through the middle decades of the 20th century, was a crucial dilemma. Western civ emerged, and gained much of its support, from a premise that it would serve social stability, that it would help anchor a unified American culture. But it was part of a discipline and a commitment to liberal education that, at their best, sought to train students in critical inquiry and inquiring objectivity. This was not an unprecedented teaching dilemma. It could even be creative. But success depended on some explicit realization of the tension involved, and given the assumptions of the program and its increasing incorporation in the memorization routines of conventional history teaching, this realization might not emerge.

Further reading

There are several really good, and critical, assessments of the origins of Western civ programs: Daniel Segal, "'Western Civ' and the Staging of History in American Higher Education," *American Historical Review* **106** (2000): 770–805; Gilbert Allardyce, "The Rise and Fall of the Western Civilization Course," *American Historical Review* **87** (1982): 695–725; David John Frank, Evan Schofer and John Torres, "Rethinking History: Change in the University Curriculum, 1910–90," *Sociology of Education* **67** (1994): 231–42; W. B. Carnochan, *The Battleground of the Curriculum: Liberal Education and American Experience* (Stanford, Calif.: Stanford University Press, 1993), esp. Chapter 6; David Shumway, *Creating American Civilization: A Genealogy of American Literature as Academic Discipline* (Minneapolis: University of Minnesota Press, 1994); on the continuing idea of Western civ as essential knowledge, Alan Bloom, *The Closing of the American Mind* (New York: Simon and Schuster, 1988); for a critique of memorization history and a plea for analysis, Peter N. Stearns, *Meaning over Memory: Recasting the Teaching of Culture and History* (Chapl Hill: University of North Carolina Press, 1993); Lawrence W. Levine, *The Opening of the American Mind: Canons, Culture, and History* (Boston: Beacon Press, 1996).

Chapter 3

The fall of Western civ, and why it still stands

In 1982, an article by Gilbert Allardyce in the *American Historical Review* (the granddaddy journal in the discipline in the United States) proclaimed the fall of the Western civ course, and a number of historians, offering ensuing commentary, largely agreed. From the 1960s onward Western civ was subjected to several related attacks. The attacks raised a number of important critical points, some of them going to the heart of the Western civ assumptions. It did indeed seem like the fortress was crumbling. But of course it did not collapse. We need to take a moment to look at the reasons for attack and at the reasons the attack did not entirely succeed (remember the US Senate vote in favor of Western civ, in 1994). Then we can return to the question of what next.

Part of the assault on Western civ simply resulted from the mood of student rebellion in the 1960s. Students protested the very idea of required courses, and many younger faculty members echoed their concerns. A number of general education programs were dismantled, and required Western civ suffered in consequence. To the extent that the Vietnam war, as it deteriorated, was seen as a Western-imperialist effort to impose power and values over a reluctant Asian people, the image of progress embodied in the Western civ vision might seem particularly tarnished.

But there were other factors as well, even more specific to Western civ and building over time. In the first place, while cherished Western civ programs existed at a number of institutions, the routine quality of many Western civ curricula had moved well away from earlier ideals – particularly when the courses were taught by reluctant graduate students and junior faculty members eager to get on to more specialized, prestigious assignments.

A large number of programs, for example, made no pretense of beginning with the origins of Western civilization, or of worrying about origins at all. Many, to be sure, dropped the Western civ label in favor of simple European history, but they still sought to benefit from a Western civ aura and, in any event, their presence unquestionably complicated any ongoing definition of Western civ. Thus many European history surveys omitted the classical period, and a significant number simply began with the modern period, around 1500 or even after. Now there is nothing wrong with a modern European history course, and lots of interesting and important things happened in Europe, and as a consequence of European causation, in the last five centuries or less. But strictly modern courses cannot possibly pretend to deal with Western civilization and some of the key issues the whole concept raises. Large numbers of surveys, furthermore, had moved away from the study of key ideas, to a diet of political narrative – the wars and kings approach to European history. By the 1980s, according to College Board soundings, the average Western civ. survey devoted twice as much time to political and diplomatic as to intellectual and cultural patterns. This approach, too, could be justified (though with greater difficulty, given the tendency to place undue emphasis on chronological memorization), but not clearly in terms of Western civilization. The battles and monarchs now highlighted had Europe as their stage, but what save geography was Western about them? The point is clear: many European survey courses had lost any Western civ impetus. Europe itself was becoming less important in world affairs and in American consciousness – in a decade when Asia seemed to command whatever attention was left over from domestic concerns. So why require a factual compendium that assumed some special European cachet?

Within the history discipline, a key development centered around the rise and growing dynamism of social history as a research approach. Here was the most dramatic innovation in historical inquiry since the rise of professional history a century before, and it inevitably had an impact on conventions in teaching. Social historians – many of them concerned with Europe, and inspired by pioneering European work in the field – argued that history should focus on ordinary people and on a wide range of human behaviors, such as crime, or leisure, or demography, and not politics or great ideas alone. In examining a classic development like the Renaissance, for example, social historians asked not about the Renaissance state or the art of Michelangelo, but about the work life and family values of workers and peasants – and they might conclude, based on these criteria, that the glittery Renaissance made little difference compared to continuities from the past or a separate set of innovations. They looked at the Protestant Reformation less as a set of purely religious changes and political struggles, and more in terms of how it altered popular education, family life, or the treatment of witchcraft. Social history, in sum, might revolutionize the way the past is evaluated.

Social history did not inevitably undermine Western civ, but in practice it disputed the Western civ tradition on several fronts. First, most social historians picked much smaller units of analysis than civilizations. Because they were dealing with new topics, and often with new kinds of source materials, they looked at individual nations or smaller regions. Only a few took a European-wide view of characteristic family structures or popular cultures (one imaginative study, for example, discussed how widely some version of the Cinderella story cropped up in folk culture, even in places outside Europe such as Siberia). Most social historians, thus, were simply not interested in Western civ. Beyond this, social historians, in paying attention to peasants, workers, or women, tended to emphasize divisions in conditions and beliefs within a society, not wholeness. What might have seemed "Western" about a group of aristocrats sitting around and discussing science, seemed much less obvious when the focus was the miserable material conditions of urban factory hands. The whole notion of Western civ as progress seemed dubious as well, when at so many points the main subject of social history involved the exploitation of peasants or the high death rates of children in the poorer classes. Social historians tended to stand some of the generalizations about Western civ on their head, arguing that they were not characteristic of the real stuff of history when the issue was ordinary people and the fabric of ordinary lives.

In practice, the addition of social history topics, such as the conditions of women, to the must-do list for history courses added to the burdens of integrating a survey course. Social history was patched into many offerings, and while this did usefully expose students to new topics it might reduce any sense of coherence. Few programs met the challenge of inserting social history into a coherent or overarching vision of what held Western civ together.

It is important to emphasize that it remains possible to reknit the link between social history and Western civ, though the relationship will at best be complex. In the 1960s, however, the much more obvious point was that social historians turned away from Western civ toward other approaches and explicitly disputed some of the Western civ assumptions about unity and progress. This was one reason many younger historians joined students in protesting about required Western civ courses. And in the radical 1960s context, many students themselves loudly wondered why Western civ courses so rarely talked about what was happening to ordinary people, why they dealt too heavily with the lifestyles of the rich and famous as if these alone comprised the past.

The onslaught on Western civ continued in the 1970s, with some newer forces joining the parade. A key development was the changing ethnic composition of the American student body, in a period when civil rights issues were loudly touted. Groups of African–American or Asian–American students often took a lead in demanding that Western civ requirements be dropped in favor of attention to other civilization traditions. Vigorous protest movement around these issues arose at places like Stanford. A few institutions – Columbia, perhaps predictably, headed the list – resisted the clamor and maintained Western civ programs without major alteration, but far more began to reduce the requirement or add other components. Stanford, for example, introduced imaginative comparative courses that would help students deal with Africa and Latin America, as well as the West, in an introductory offering.

And these changes, in turn, fed the growing movement to substitute world history for Western civ, and to insist that "real" world history involved an escape from West-centered curricula that at best made a few new gestures to other parts of the world. A first generation of world history textbooks and advocacies in the 1960s had not made much headway against Western civ. But by the late 1970s conditions had changed. The new characteristics of the American student body, the undeniable decline of Europe in world affairs, and the equally undeniable influence of various regions and global forces on the United States, added up to a powerful argument for a new approach to the history survey, at both high school and college levels. Furthermore, some explicit research in world history made it clear that significant analytical issues could be pursued in a world history context, and some new teacher-training programs emerged as well. Interestingly, the leadership in world history came not from the Ivy League institutions, that tended still to favor a Western civ approach, but from less prestigious centers that were, it might be argued, closer to student demand. But a number of leading historians became involved in the movement, which generated a new professional association and journal and showed every sign of increasing vigor.

Finally, by the 1980s, changes in literary and historical study associated with what was called "postmodernism" could also challenge the Western civ tradition. Postmodernists tended to argue against any absolute standards or fixed canons in historical research, and Western civ had certainly become canonical. If truth is relative, how was it possible to define and defend a fixed set of Western values? Postmodernism had greater impact in English than in history departments, and its influence in history survey teaching was limited. Still, it added to the climate in which many scholars – some gleefully, others with real regret – proclaimed the "fall" of Western civ as an American teaching icon.

But Western civ did not fall. Many colleges have retained or reintroduced a Western civ requirement. State standards for high school students in the history area have maintained a high Western civ content, though rarely under an exclusive label. The Advanced Placement program in European history (again, not exactly Western civ but often sharing and promoting its cachets) has grown. To be sure, a new AP world history came into existence in 2002, and long-run competitive prospects were not clear; but in the short run it was anticipated that both programs would continue to grow. Western civ was no longer the only bull in the ring, but it had not definitively yielded its claims.

There were several reasons for this. Many history teachers, because of sincere conviction or because of the limitations of busy schedules and some routine-mindedness, resist conversion away from Western civ. Developing a world history survey alternative, for example, is a fair amount of work and a jolt to established preconceptions, and these do not come easily. In the 1980s and 1990s also, historical research was swept by a new level of interest in cultural issues – what some labeled the "cultural turn" – and this might complement a Western civ approach more comfortably than some of the earlier versions of social history.

But forces outside the discipline were particularly responsible for the explicit counterattack in Western civ's name. Conservatism was on the rise in American political life from Ronald Reagan's 1980 election onward, complete with new and potent think tanks such as the Heritage Foundation. Distrustful of liberal professors, who undeniably dominated most major history departments, conservatives sought to highlight the damage they claimed recent intellectual trends had caused and to find ways of asserting their own grip on higher education. Under one Reagan-appointed head of the National Endowment for the Humanities, for example, social history projects were virtually banned from federal funding. On the more positive side, and doubtless in most cases out of sincere conviction, conservative educational leaders sought to reinvigorate the Western civ tradition as against more permissive curricula and world history alternatives alike.

There were two main arguments. First, countering the mood of the 1960s, a new generation of educational leaders – not all of them politically conservative – argued that a good education should include some standard requirements. A return to a core curriculum was a widely-heeded rallying cry. And second, conservative educators truly believed that the superiority of Western values was such that students must be exposed to them explicitly, in order to create an educated and coherent citizenry.

The first point – the pleas for the reestablishment of requirements – did not of course necessarily involve Western civ. One could have, and some institutions did have, a general education program with world history or, heaven forefend, no history. But most people, if only for knee-jerk reasons, still associated Western civ with the idea of core. Several books appeared in the 1980s, insisting on the need to know a host of facts, mainly about Western history, in order to qualify as an educated person, which made the connections with a Western civ requirement quite explicit, if also dauntingly mindless. Here was a new conservative game: claim that present-day young people were shockingly ignorant of Western history facts, without demonstrating that this mattered much, or that previous young people had known any more. And then insist that Western civ requirements return. On a more general level, almost all of the new plans for reconstituting a core, whether from individual educators or "blue ribbon" commissions, included a Western civ component.

The second point demanded more careful phrasing, for few conservative educators were brash enough to wish to slam other civilization traditions explicitly. In this sense, the context had changed significantly since the blithe superiority assumptions of James Robinson and his colleagues. But there was no question of the depth and sincerity of the continuing conviction that West was best. As one proponent put it, absurdly and inaccurately: students should only study Western civilization because Western civilization is the only tradition that tolerates others. Other advocates insisted on the importance of providing students with heroic leadership examples and inspiring principles through history, and in turn on the centrality of Western history to this provision. In this vision, not only world history but also social history were banished to the educational sidelines. Pushing Western civ might also allow conservative advocates to flush out campus liberals, for academic institutions did not docilely blend with the new political trends in the nation as a whole.

Put the two points together, the need for requirement and the essential qualities of the West, and the case could be powerful. Alan Bloom, a University of Chicago philosopher, wrote of the "closing" of the American mind because of (among other things) the declining commitment to a Western core. Others urged the vital need for a recommitment to the West to save American education from the depths of purgatory.

Conservatives naturally respond to tradition, and Western civ certainly fits that category. But there was more involved than this general association. Many of the conservatives who surged forward in the 1980s were profoundly hostile to the culture of the 1960s, with its overtones of radicalism and permissiveness. Insistence on core values and, in education, on core require- ments was a direct response to the real or imagined excesses of the earlier decade, and, of course, Western civ figured logically in a number of ways. Many conservatives claimed, often with little or no evidence, that the educational achievements of American young people had deteriorated thanks to the pedagogical experiments of the 1960s. The tendency to promote memorization lists, where college students often displayed major gaps in knowledge, was part of this general approach. There was no reason to think, in fact, that students of earlier generations would have done any better, and there were real questions as to the value of the lists in the first place. But there was a deep sense that American youth was moving away from a grasp of vital knowledge and vital discipline alike, which is why both requirements and an insistence on a traditional approach to history, Western civ at its head, seemed imperative.

The renewed appeal for Western civ also revived two of the motives that had prompted the course in the first place, almost a century before. The need to provide a common heritage to students in an age of unprecedented immigration was palpable. While the percentage of the American population that was foreign born was lower than around 1900, the absolute numbers were much larger. And the sources of immigration were far more diverse, including people from various parts of Asia, the Caribbean and Latin America. While some observers were eager to embrace Latin Americans within Western civilization (a debatable point, as we will later discuss), far more immigrants clearly originated outside this orbit than had occurred in American history since the days of the African slave trade. A large Muslim minority grew, along with many people of Hindu, Buddhist, or Confucian background. Here was a situation in which concerns about Americanization (though this term was no longer used) increased. Requiring such a diverse student body to acquire knowledge of Western civ, and perhaps even a sense that it was part of their heritage as new Americans, seemed as vital as it had back in the days of Robinson's "new history." Conservatives were edgy about diversity, and sought ways to use education to reduce their concerns.

The world at large was changing also, and this too could set conservative teeth on edge. The end of the Cold War, by 1991, in one sense reduced the fears that the United States and its Western allies were under attack. But the Cold War was replaced by the growing pressures of globalization, which might make any civilization, even a powerful one, fear for its identity. New rivalries with Islamic militants created another source of concern. China's expanding economic strength suggested yet another competitive force for the future. The United States was touted as the only remaining superpower. But the future was hardly secure, and the ability to refer to a Western tradition might provide comfort amid the new global challenges and complexities.

A number of factors thus underlay the otherwise surprising passion for the maintenance or restoration of Western civ programs. Many advocates sincerely believed that strong Western civ requirements were essential to deal with concerns ranging from wayward youth to radical faculty members to anxieties about the national and global future at a time of rapid change. This advocacy combined with the heritage of established educational routines and with memories of the undeniable charms of Western history. And so Western civ hung on, even reenergized, despite the several good reasons for its decline.

In the long run, as was argued earlier, Western civ will probably fade further, particularly as teachers gain more experience with world history alternatives. But for the moment, there are two obvious problems: first, a considerable division over what kinds of survey history make sense for contemporary education; and second, a conservative appropriation of Western civ that may not do full justice to the tradition itself. Are there ways out of the dilemma, ways to reduce the culture wars atmosphere surrounding the history component of basic education?

Not surprisingly, a number of imaginative proposals have been advanced, seeking to bridge between the camps of world versus Western history. One historian, coming from the Western civ side with real recognition of the need to broaden to the wider world, urges that a four-semester college program is the answer: a two-semester sequence in Western civ, but also a semester course on some "non-Western" civ and a semester course on 20th century world history. The argument is vigorous, but it is not clear that the solution is sound. In the first place, it would not really please the world history advocates, because it still gives centrality to Western civ; the term "non-Western" itself is a giveaway that students are meant to think of the world in terms organized primarily by the Western experience. In the second place, much as we all love history, it is not realistic to assume that most college programs have space for four required history courses (quite apart from the sticky question of what would happen to US history in the process).

We may yet figure out some good ways to sequence world and Western civ courses. Historians have not been particularly adept in creating relationships between one level of history and another; there is a tendency to start all over again each time a survey course rolls around. We could do better, particularly for students exposed to college as well as high school programs.

But the answer to the dilemmas surrounding the place of Western civ does not lie in course combinations alone. We also need to think through some of the basic assumptions involved in Western civ, as they have accumulated through several decades of experience and in recognition of the fact that, from its inception, Western civ programs were meant to serve more purposes than providing just another history course.

Happily, world history really does provide an opportunity for this analysis. Most world history courses give considerable space to the stories of major civilizations. There are a few dissenters, in courses that focus only on global forces – such as trade patterns, diseases, or migrations. But even the global forces advocates usually acknowledge that the forces are experienced by societies with varied geographies and histories – by different civilizations, in fact. And the two other common approaches to world history, comparing major societies or examining significant contacts among societies, explicitly assume a civilization model. There is ample room in the world history course for attention to the key issues that Western civ involves, without distorting the other purposes of the course, or the treatment of the other societies and the larger forces that must be offered. And indeed, all the major textbooks in world history, including the several that are rated as truly global, give considerable space to data about Western civ. What they do not always do, and what this essay seeks to offer, is to highlight some of the central questions about what Western civilization was and is. Partly because they do not want to seem to be singling Western civilization out, partly because the leading publishers still insist on a good bit of conventional Western coverage with no questions asked, partly because some of the assumptions about Western civ lie beneath the surface, many world history courses lay out facts about the Western past without sufficient analysis really to bridge between the newer world history approach and the Western civ tradition. It is an analysis that can and should be informed by testing some of the assumptions that have supported Western civ programs for decades, and that have permeated the recent conservative advocacy as well. The issues involved are complicated, which is why the questions will be easier to pose than the answers, but the challenge is exhilarating. We can pick out new contours, even find some new meanings, by flying over familiar terrain.

Further reading

On forces attacking Western civ traditions: Howard Brick, *Age of Contradiction: American Thought and Culture in the 1960s* (New York: Twayne Publishers; London: Prentice Hall International, 1998); Craig Lockard, "World History and the Public: The National Standards Debates," http://www.theaha.org/Perspectives/issues/2000; Edmund Burke, III, "Marshall G. S. Hodgson and the hemispheric interregional approach to world history," *Journal of World History* 6 (1996): 237–49; Daniel Segal, ed., *Crossing Cultures: Essays in the Displacement of Western Civilization* (Tucson: University of Arizona Press, 1992); Harland Bloland, "Postmodernism and higher education," *Journal of Higher Education* 66 (1995) 521–59; Robert Proctor, *Defining the Humanities: How Rediscovering a Tradition Can Improve Our Schools: With a Curriculum for Today's Students* (Bloomington: Indiana University Press, 1998); Francis Schaeffer, *How Should We Then Live? The Rise and Decline of Western Thought and Culture* (Westchester, Ill.: Crossway Books, 1983); Ralph Hancock, *America, The West and Liberal Education* (Lanham, Md.: Rowman & Littlefield, 1999); on compromise proposals: Betty Schmitz, *Core Curriculum and Cultural Pluralism: A Guide for Campus Planners* (Washington, DC: Association of American Colleges, c1992); Jerry Gaff, *General Education: The Changing Agenda* (Washington, DC: Association of American Colleges and Universities, 1999); Michael Boyle, " 'Hisperanto': Western Civilization in the Global Curriculum," http://www. theaha.org/Perspectives/issues/1998; Chester Finn, ed., *Against Mediocracy: The Humanities in America's High Schools* (New York: Holmes & Meier, 1984). For a more general conservative use of the West: Patrick Buchanan, *Death of the West: How Dying Populations and Immigrant Invasions Imperil our Country and Civilization* (New York: St. Martin's Press, 2002).

Part II

Getting Western
civilization started

Chapters in this section first take up some definitional questions essential in dealing with civilizations, and then some fundamental issues involved in identifying Western civilization itself. These issues are partly comparative, in juxtaposing Western civ with other "civs," and partly chronological, starting with the obvious problem of when Western civ began.

Chapter 4

Defining civilizations

Most world historians use the concept of civilization, as noted in the last chapter, but many are uncomfortable with it. In contrast, the Western civ tradition, launched by scholars such as Robinson, tended to rest on assumptions that civilization had obvious meaning, as it contrasted with other, clearly inferior, types of human existence. Clearly, in order to deal with Western civilization sensibly, in a contemporary context, we need to spend a moment on the noun, before we turn to the adjective.

Civilization has two meanings in world history. First, it describes a form of human organization. Second, it describes certain coherences that develop in certain regions as the basis for particular civilizations.

As a form of human organization, civilizations grow up in economies – all of them, initially, primarily agricultural – that generate considerable economic surplus. These economies may go through bad times, associated with failed harvests, and they can harbor massive poverty, but in most years there is enough surplus to support a relatively complex social and political structure and, often, some expensive cultural monuments.

Civilizations also have cities. Some cities can crop up in societies that are not otherwise civilizations, but civilizations produce more cities and more urban influence than other societies. It is vital to note that, in agricultural civilizations, most people remain rural. But cities capture a good bit of the economic surplus. They reflect and encourage trade, sending manufactured products and political services out in return for food. They usually promote additional cultural activities.

Most civilizations have writing. This allows record-keeping, which facilitates commercial transactions and political bureaucracies. Writing also provides new ways to record knowledge and so may promote new kinds of intellectual activities. Again, in most civilizations until recently, the majority of people remain illiterate. But writing is an important social tool nevertheless.

Civilizations, finally, have formal states. Many societies can organize quite well without formal states, depending on local groupings and individual leaders. This is obviously true in most hunting and gathering societies, but there are state-less agricultural societies as well. States have some bureaucracies (even if quite small) as well as identified leadership.

Civilization, as a form of human organization, is not necessarily better than other forms. It often involves more social inequality than other forms. It may not produce more kindness or happiness. If by civilized we mean the capacity to be polite or altruistic, then it is vital to note that many non-civilized societies produce more courteous and generous people than many civilizations do. (Western civilization, as we will see, was long known as being rather crude.) Many civilizations, to be sure, look down on other societies as rude and primitive; some of these prejudices informed the early definitions of Western civilization. But we need to try to detach implications of superiority from the idea of civilization. Furthermore, many successful societies long continued without civilization. Herding societies in Central Asia, for example, thrived without the trappings of civilization until relatively recent centuries.

Most world historians would grant that Western civilization easily passes the definition test for civilization as a form of organization: it had cities, writing, states, social inequality, and surpluses. They would only urge that this does not mean that the West had therefore gained some edge over other kinds of societies, in terms of the quality of human existence. And they would insist that we remember to pay serious attention to other kinds of societies along with our focus on developments in places like the West.

The second meaning of civilization focuses on coherence, and this aspect of the definition is crucial to the exploration of Western civ. Very early civilizations were usually confined to fairly small regions, often along river valleys where extra coordination made economic sense. But with time, some civilizations produced surplus populations, and increased military power, and in some cases offered attractive institutions and values, and so they tended to expand. Expansion frequently generated various kinds of conflict, but in the long run successful, enlarged civilizations spread enough common institutions and cultural values, and often shared trading systems and social patterns, to create a certain amount of coherence throughout the expanded region.

The establishment of Chinese civilization, between about 600 BCE and 200 CE, forms the clearest example of this process. Northern China, where civilization as a type of human organization had first taken hold in this region, linked to southern China, through a mix of trade, conquest, and deliberate migrations. Chinese leaders worked hard to integrate the expanded empire by providing a common elite language (Mandarin), a set of centralized political institutions under the emperor and bureaucracy, and a common elite culture defined particularly by Confucianism. As a result there is no big problem in talking about Chinese civilization in terms of several kinds of coherence. Even gender relations took on a "Chinese" quality thanks to shared beliefs and politics.

Even in China, to be sure, coherence should not be pressed too far. Rich people often connected more easily to the shared institutions and values than poor people did. Regional differences remained, and frontier zones were often only loosely linked to the main civilization (a situation that remains true today in China). There were sometimes racial or cultural minorities within the civilization that did not fully integrate. Chinese civilization did not mean that all Chinese people shared the same set of values or the same relationship to dominant political institutions.

Civilizations could also change. One of the really tricky aspects of using the civilization concept to designate coherences involves preventing it from becoming too rigid at one extreme, while also making sure that it still has some bearing over time. To have any useful meaning, civilizations should retain some identifiable features for many centuries. If a society totally changes stripes every fifty years, this would be important and fascinating but would probably swamp the civilization concept. In China, for example, it is legitimate to define an unusually strong interest in political order from about 500 BCE onward. This entered into characteristic political institutions and into Confucian culture alike, and it survives into the 21st century even though the traditional empire and formal Confucianism are both long gone. But China in the early 21st century, or even in the 15th century, is much different from the China of 200 CE. Change and continuity operate in an important tension as part of the civilization concept when extended over time.

Now, when it comes to coherences, Western civilization, rather than being unusually obvious, actually raises some unusual problems. This does not mean that the concept is invalid; but it does mean that assumptions about a simple narrative for the Western story, à la James Harvey Robinson, are really off the mark.

Most obviously, Western civilization almost never even came close to political unity. This is not unprecedented; Indian civilization was rarely united either. It is quite possible for a civilization to develop coherences in terms of shared values, trade networks, and some common political and social patterns. But there is no question that the coherences are more challenging when there is almost no shared political experience – and no question that, objectively, Western civ is harder to define, at almost any time period, than Chinese civilization is. We will also see that Western civilization moved around geographically more than most civilizations did. Again, this is not an insuperable problem, but it adds to the need to be very explicit about defining Westernness, rather than taking it for granted.

The change aspect is a challenge as well. One world historian once argued that Western civilization had a greater capacity to change than did most other civilizations, and that this is really one of its defining features. This is worth debating. But, if true, it means that seeking the continuity aspect of Western civilization becomes particularly important, unless we should decide to talk about one Western civilization after another, Western civilizations rather than Western civ.

Different civilizations fall into different places on the coherence scale. Chinese civilization and, later, Middle Eastern/North African Islamic civilization are probably on the high side. This does not mean that they are better civilizations than others, just a bit easier to define from their points of origin onward. On the hard-to-define side comes Japan – was it a separate civilization or, because of its conscious imitation, a distinctive part of a larger East Asian civilization that had China as its progenitor? Or Latin America or Russia, which copy or have imposed so many elements from other civilizations but may nevertheless have definable civilizational identities of their own. Western civ is probably in the middle, in this scale of analytical difficulty, though a bit harder to identify on the whole than Indian civilization.

This means that Western civ, far from being a story that can be captured by moving from one factual memorization task to another, is a set of questions, an invitation to analysis and to debate.

And there is one other point about civilizations in general. All major civilizations – major in terms of covering a significant geographical area and lasting a considerable period of time – are by definition successful. Western civilization clearly takes its rank here but so do several other traditions. Some civilizations are also going to seem more recognizable, and possibly better, depending on how closely they fit our own value systems. Since Western civ is "home" to many Americans, it will be constantly tempting to see it as best. This is an understandable reaction, but it is not too useful analytically. Indeed, it can be positively misleading. This book is not intended to wean anyone away from Western values, whatever they prove to be. It is intended, however, as a treatment of Western values historically rather than editorially. Some of the coherences that often defined the West are not in fact very attractive. Others seems weird or objectionable to people from other traditions. We need to be able to capture a range of reactions as part of our quest for what Western civ has been and is.

Further reading

Brian Fagin, *Africa in the Iron Age: c. 500 B.C. to A.D. 1400* (Cambridge; New York: Cambridge University Press, 1995); Anatoly M. Khazanov, *Nomads and the Outside World* (Madison: University of Wisconsin Press, 1984).

Chapter 5

When in the world is Western civilization?

It is quite difficult to decide when Western civ began, though debating the question of origins is rewarding and interesting. We have seen that the initial Western civ tradition, launched by Robinson, assumed that the answer to the question of origins was virtually automatic: there is a single story from the ancient river valley societies onward. What should have been discussed and worried about, here, was simply assumed. As Western civ courses have evolved, taking realities like length of semester into account, different beginning points have been decided upon. Again, however, the tendency has been just to get started, rather than to debate. Here, if briefly, we debate.

There are really three choices, and one of them is pretty clearly not worth too much attention. Choice 1, with Robinson, ancient Mesopotamia and Egypt. This is the bad one. Choice 2, with lots of scholars and many of the conservative proponents of Western civ today, is classical Greece and Rome. Choice 3, my own preference, but again only with careful justification, involves the Middle Ages, after Rome's collapse in the West.

I. The West as ancient

Many societies have claimed roots that go farther back than they can definitely prove; ancient lineage adds luster and legitimacy. Thus Jews claim a much older history than can be definitely established – the first definite reference to the Jewish people dates from 1100 BCE, well after the presumed Exodus from Egypt. Chinese intellectuals long pointed to ancient dynasties from which core Chinese values presumably emanated. Here, too, the stories were not necessarily untrue, they were simply not clearly true.

The idea of tracing Western civilization back to ancient Mesopotamia and Egypt is obviously attractive, for the claim implies that Western civ is the oldest one in operation. Other societies might be dismissed as upstarts compared to the Western ancestry.

And several points are clear. First, Mesopotamia and then Egypt are the oldest civilizations on record, with civilization defined as in the previous chapter. Their achievements are not only early, but also truly impressive.

There is every reason to study both societies for what they reveal about the range of human accomplishment. Second, there are links between Mesopotamia and Egypt and the civilization that later sprang up in Greece, and from this, in turn, to Rome and on to Western civilization. In this sense, Robinson was right in claiming a continuous story – and his claims persist, echoed in the many high school texts and the smaller percentage of college courses that duly begin the Western story back in the river valleys of the Middle East and North Africa.

But the dangers of this claim clearly outweigh the reality of any story line. I have heard reports of American teachers telling students that civilization has steadily moved west, from its inception in the Middle East to the glories of the United States today. The idea is profoundly nonsensical, totally ignoring Asian and African history and distorting the Western record itself.

The problem is that neither Egypt nor Mesopotamia was Western. This is obvious geographically, though, of course, civilizational values and institutions can move from place to place so the location point is not decisive. It remains important to note that, during most of the time that the river valley civilizations flourished, most of Western Europe was just beginning to learn about agriculture, much less about civilization as a form of human organization. Two other, more decisive factors are: first, while building blocks were introduced in Egypt and Mesopotamia that would be used in later civilizations, the essential coherences were not. And second, the legacy of Egypt and Mesopotamia did not devolve primarily on the West, but (understandably enough) on the Middle East and North Africa themselves, and to some extent on eastern Europe and other parts of Africa. The idea that there is a direct or special line from the river valleys to the West is truly misleading.

The Middle East would inherit far more from the river valley civilizations than Western Europe did. Thus the practice of veiling women in public, revived under Islam, first developed in ancient Mesopotamia. There is no heritage in such an intensely personal area to be discovered in the West. Yet we do not normally trace contemporary Middle Eastern civilization back to 3500 BCE (when Mesopotamian civilization first took shape) but rather to the rise of Islam, which gave the civilization the decisive shape that it retains in many ways today. Why do more for Western Europe, where the links are far more tenuous anyway?

From either the ancient Middle East or ancient Egypt, before 800 BCE (in some cases well before), came writing; the use of iron and other technologies such as the wheel; the idea of money; the idea of written laws. These civilizational tools spread from their points of origin to other parts of Asia and Africa and to Europe, beginning with eastern Europe. They never had to be reinvented by any of the civilizations that later arose in this orbit, including the West. Tools of this sort were vital, but they are also in many ways neutral; almost any civilization can use them, and many did. A civilization is not defined by the fact that it has writing or laws or money.

Civilizations are usually defined by some combination of distinctive features in politics, society, and culture – and this is what we will look for in discussing the real origins of Western civ. Both Mesopotamia and Egypt had fascinating, complex societies, states and cultures – but they were not Western. The most characteristic government forms and political ideas that would ultimately develop in the West had virtually nothing to do with the states of Egypt or Babylon. It is true that, very briefly, the Roman emperors, having conquered Egypt, took on some of the trappings of Egyptian pharaohs, including a claim to divinity. But this was a brief and frankly uncharacteristic moment. While Western states benefited from a few of the implements that had first emerged in ancient politics, their civilizational flavor had to be independently invented later. The same holds for major social forms.

Culture is, admittedly, just a bit trickier. There have been some vigorous debates in recent years about the influence of Egypt and Mesopotamia on Greek culture. Martin Bernal claimed that racist blinders have prevented Westerners from seeing how much Greece borrowed from Africa and West Asia, while respondents like Lefkowitz have vigorously asserted the essential novelty of the Greek achievement. On the whole, the debate has generated more heat than light.

What is clear is that we have to expand the "tools" heritage a bit in dealing with Greek culture (leaving aside for a moment the extent to which Greek is Western). Greece gained not only the idea of writing, but a specific Phoenician alphabet, a great improvement over Mesopotamian cuneiform, from which it developed its own lettering and which in turn inspired Roman letters – the alphabet of the West.

From Egypt came architectural forms much studied by the Greeks, and which helped inspire Greek monuments (which, however, were quite different in detail and actually inferior in engineering accomplishment).

From an offshoot of the ancient civilizations came the Jewish religion that was of tremendous importance in later inspiring and shaping Christianity – but also Islam; there was no exclusive heritage here. Much of Western history would be defined in some small part by hatred of the Jews, but this should not minimize the relevance of Jewish innovations to later religious history throughout Europe, North Africa, and the Middle East. And Jewish writings themselves benefited from earlier Mesopotamian stories, such as the idea of a great flood; this, too, would enter the Western cultural storehouse, and other storehouses as well.

From Egypt, particularly, came mathematical and scientific discoveries picked up by the Greeks, whose own scientific tradition would prove so deeply and durably influential. But here we can begin to be a bit more precise about the difference between a significant cultural heritage and the kind of continuity one would look for in a civilization. Later Greek scientists like Anaximander (610–546 BCE) did indeed carefully study Egyptian thought.

Mathematicians went to Egypt to study. Indeed, Egyptian mathematics and astronomy were superior to anything the Greeks themselves achieved. But Greeks such as Anaximander added a vital component to scientific thinking that the Egyptians had lacked: the idea of a cosmos, a natural system in which the earth operated. Egyptians, who looked at the stars as emblems of past pharaoh-gods and at the heavens as divine, simply had no interest in, or capacity for, generalizing about nature. They had no explicit scientific philosophy. This key feature of what would become a Western scientific characteristic had yet to be introduced.

The science and mathematics point is admittedly tricky. A lot of Western civ emphasis has gone into an argument that, not much simplified, runs like this. There was no science before Greece and its heroic achievements (the origins of Western rationalism *à la* Robinson again). Then after Greece faded science, too, became moribund, until revived in the rejuvenated West, which then reintroduced science to a strangely sleepy world. We will take up the second part of this fable later on. For now, it is vitally important to acknowledge the great achievements of the societies that preceded Greece – Egypt, for example, first introduced fractions – to which Greece would owe a great deal, so that we do not overdo the originality of the Greek achievement. It is still possible to argue that there was a Greek contribution, which again highlights the extent to which Egypt and Mesopotamia were not Western.

The overall point is clear, in culture and certainly in politics: the Western story does not really start as early as is sometimes imagined. We risk sacrificing any real analysis of coherences in Western civilization by claiming such ambitious historical roots. (And, of course, we also risk ignoring the extent to which other civilization traditions also utilized the same roots.)

2. Greece and Rome

The second option for determining the origins of Western civilization has much more plausibility, and, of course, it has been warmly supported by generations of intellectuals since before the Renaissance. Western origins lie in Greece and Rome. Here again, we are dealing with great civilizations whose achievements might add luster to the definitions of Western civilization. Here also, without question, we are dealing with memories and memorials that form part of the Western identity. What educated person in the West cannot identify a structure like the Roman Coliseum as "ours"? Yet, despite assumptions and vicarious credit-seeking, it is surely legitimate to ask what was "Western" about Greece and Rome, or rather what Greek and Roman innovations proved to be a durable part of the coherences of Western civilization.

For there are two or three problems. In the first place, particularly for Greece but to an extent Rome as well, the major accomplishments that survived were not exclusively, or even primarily, part of a Western heritage.

Greece was not located in what became the West, though it did plant some Western colonies and has itself become Western in the past 30 years. Greek leaders looked eastward, not westward. Other than raw materials and food supplies, there was nothing to seek in the West. Thus when Alexander the Great set out to build an empire, he built in Asia and North Africa. There was no contact with the West at all, and Alexander proved quite willing to make compromises with Greek political and even cultural principles in order to form a more durable West Asian amalgam. Too much emphasis on classical Greece as "Western" really distorts what the Greeks themselves thought.

Furthermore, the Greek legacy fed ongoing traditions in Eastern Europe and even in the Middle East more than in the West. Western civilization owes to the Greeks, but it cannot look to classical Greece as "theirs," in the sense of providing an exclusive badge of Western identity. Aristotle was a philosopher appropriated by the Arabs, the Byzantines and later even the Russians, just as he was appropriated by West Europeans (who bowed in part to the reputation they learned from Arab and Byzantine sources). Classical Greek architectural styles influenced Turkey and Russia, just as they influenced France and the United States. All of this means that if Greece can usefully be regarded as a Western progenitor – and it surely was in part – it was not just a Western progenitor. It is profoundly misleading to think of a straight line from Greece to the West, as though the purpose of Greek history was to provide key ingredients for the Western recipe.

And there is another problem, this one involving Rome as well as Greece. Greece and Rome combined were not as recognizably Western as, say, classical China or classical India are recognizably Chinese or Indian. Western Europe stands in relation to classical Greece much as Japan stands to classical China: a heavy borrower, but not clearly a direct civilizational heir (and one would never think of beginning a history of Japanese civilization with detailed developments in classical China).

The question of linkage is what we have to explore. There is very little connection, for starters, between Greek and Roman society and later Western social forms. There is significant but incomplete connection between Greek and Roman culture and later Western cultural forms. Politics sits in the middle, with some unquestionable relevance to what became the Western political tradition, but some real discontinuities as well.

What is involved here partly reflects the difference in geography. The West built itself in places different from Greek strongholds and partly different from Roman centers. But the key disconnect results from the deep rifts caused by the collapse of the Roman empire in the West. It was impossible to keep Rome and its Greek legacy going. It was impossible even to revive many aspects of Rome when things got better. In China, by contrast, the end of a classical empire (the Han dynasty) led to several centuries of political chaos, but enough capacity and memory remained that most key features of Han politics and culture could then be restored, by the 6th century CE. This was simply not the case in the West.

And this means that many features of Greece and Rome that did ultimately enter the Western experience came as very selective imitations, not direct survivals or thorough revivals. The imitations underline the extent to which Greece and Rome were essential to the Western tradition, but also the extent to which they, themselves, were not fully Western. The connecting links are jagged at best, possibly broken. Which is why there is legitimate debate.

Linkages in the social sphere are particularly hard to find. Greece and Rome had aristocracies, merchants, peasants – but so did most agricultural civilizations, including Western Europe later on and China and India at the time. The same holds true concerning patriarchal conditions for women. Some of the most distinctive social structures in Greece and Rome – such as the relatively large rural villages in places like Sicily – turn out to be characteristic of the Mediterranean region (east as well as west, including parts of North Africa) more than of Western Europe which was not primarily Mediterranean. Slavery was a vivid social feature in both Greece and Rome, though it included people engaged in household service, tutoring, and commerce as well as agricultural and mine workers. While some slavery would survive in Western Europe after Rome fell, it did not become a characteristic social feature of Western civilization generally. Nor is there much relationship between merchants' positions and values in Greece and Rome and those that became more central to Western civilization later on. And while long after Rome's fall some Western aristocrats would seek to participate extensively in classical culture, the foundations of the Western aristocracy were quite different from those of Greece and Rome. Although aristocrats in the classical period, and later in the West, stressed military virtues, there was a great difference between Greco–Roman and later Western aristocratic methods of war, the latter based primarily on cavalry, the former on leading foot soldiers as servants of the state.

Roman law did help codify certain kinds of social relationships. When Roman law was revived in Western Europe, by the 11th and 12th centuries, it could have some influence on male–female relationships or concepts of property. Even Roman slave law, while it had little impact within later Western Europe, influenced legal arrangements for slaves, and cultural concepts of slavery, when Europeans began enslaving Africans in the Americas. So there are linkages, but not primarily in terms of direct continuities between classical society and the social forms more commonly associated with Western civilization. Indeed, a really continuous Western social history began on the ashes of Rome's collapse, around very localized agricultural estates and the peasant–landlord relations that ensued, rather than within the classical period itself.

The same disconnect applies to many aspects of popular culture. Few Western games or songs or folk stories originated in the classical period (in contrast, for example, to popular football, forms of which go back to Middle Ages). A few Roman holidays survived in altered forms, particularly the celebrations around the winter solstice that would later inform aspects of Christmas. Influenced by Christianity, characteristic Western ideas about sexuality and, even more obviously, homosexuality differed greatly from predominant beliefs in Greece and Rome. Historians have disputed over whether Western distaste for homosexuality took shape when Rome fell or a bit later on, but there is no question that Greco–Roman acceptance of homo-sexual arrangements as part of upper-class lifestyle did not become part of the Western canon – though the tradition may have held on just a bit better in Italy, closer to Roman traditions, than farther north.

Culture and social arrangements combined in Greece and Rome to produce a considerable lack of interest in improvements in production technology. There is no need to associate Western civilization too closely with technological innovation – lest it seem purely modern. But the more sluggish Greco–Roman stance differed from what came later. Several promising inventions were sketched but ignored. Philosophers argued that technology was unworthy of pure science. The reliance on slaves reduced concern about technological improvements in production (in contrast to the Roman inventiveness in areas of civil engineering).

The overwhelming fact in the cultural sphere was the lack of a major, compelling popular religion within the Greco–Roman tradition. Civic religious festivals and beliefs in the panoply of gods and goddesses were truly important to many people in Greece and Rome. Many ordinary folk added additional beliefs and worship practices, around more emotional or mystery religions. And vestiges of all this doubtless survived into the spread of Christianity. Christian churches, for example, were often located on the sites of Roman temples, both because of available building materials and as a means of capturing some established veneration. But there was not much connection. Western civilization would gain its first clear unity through Christian culture, and this was not a survival from the popular culture that had characterized most of the Greco–Roman era.

High culture, of course, is another matter. Christian thought did assimilate important aspects of Greek and Roman philosophy. Greek science, with its emphasis on broad philosophical generalizations about the cosmos, was *the* science for the West once it began to be rediscovered in the 11th century until the 17th century; and even after that point, some of its principles, including the quest for a logical natural universe, still applied. For more centuries than was entirely healthy, Western science would consist of slavishly utilizing Greek anatomy textbooks, geometry treatises and the like – errors (including, in astronomy, the late Greek belief that the sun revolves around the earth) and all.

Again, some cautions are essential about Greek science. Science strongly influenced wider Greek philosophy, but a scientific outlook was not widely shared, certainly by ordinary people. It was not greatly reflected even in Greek literature. We have seen, further, that Greek science built heavily on earlier achievements, and that the Greeks did not in fact catch up with predecessors such as the Egyptians in some aspects of mathematics. Finally, even as Greek science did advance, important scientific traditions were also developing in other classical civilizations, notably India and China; there was no Greek monopoly here, which means that undue emphasis on some early Western rational spark is really off the mark. Chinese science, particularly, with strong links to technology, generated more practical findings at this point than did Greek. None of this erases the idea of some legacy, but a balanced perspective is important.

The idea of legacy is more straightforward when it comes to high art. Greek and Roman building styles – later known, revealingly, as the classical style – continued to influence Western public buildings of various sorts – and indeed they still do so today. Other styles came in to compete, notably medieval Gothic, but classical modes often set the standard. Traditions of classical sculpture were more often disputed, but they remained influential. Painting styles, more evanescent, saw less continuity. But in drama, specific Greek plays plus the rules Greeks formulated for drama retained a durable hold. There were some disruptions after Rome fell, because Christians objected to some aspects of classical high culture and because the decline of cities and commerce reduced the funding available for cultural production, but there is no reason to dispute a deep connection between many aspects of classical art and an ongoing Western tradition. The connection persisted whether through the direct reenactment of Greek drama or poetry, or the influence that showed through in the themes and styles of later Western authors such as Shakespeare or Racine. Again, even in high culture, the religious centerpiece was missing, for the gods and goddesses yielded to Christianity, and this meant some real changes in the subject matter of art even when classical forms were used. But a dynamic linkage existed. A significant part of Western high culture was born with Greece and Rome.

So: high culture yes, popular culture, religion, and characteristic social forms largely no. A complex scorecard, which suggests the obvious: that the origins of Western civilization are unusually complex (in part because of Rome's fall) compared to the great Asian civilizations; and that real debate is based in part on what index one uses to measure what a civilization is.

But there may be a tiebreaker, in politics and political forms; and this is also where some of the most revealing confusions about Western origins show through. Greece and Rome had a variety of political forms. One result was a great deal of writing about politics, debating the various merits of aristocratic versus tyrannical versus democratic rule. Here was another vital legacy for the West, connected to other aspects of high culture: an emphasis on political thought and an ability to discuss several structures in principle. This is a key reason, in turn, why so many Western political terms, regardless of specific language, come from Roman and particularly Greek roots. Rome also produced an empire, and while land-based empires were *not* characteristic Western political forms, as things turned out, the memory of imperial greatness played a role in Western civilization (though also in East European civilization, where it actually made more sense given the direct connection between the Roman and the Byzantine Empires). Rome also developed an emphasis on law and legal codifications, and while these were lost for a time in the West they were later recovered and played an undeniable political role.

But most of the characteristic features of Greco–Roman political life and institutions were not passed on to later Western civilization; the active political legacy was real but limited. During much of the Greco–Roman era the preferred government form was a city-state dominated by the aristocracy, and while this form would reappear later on in Italy, it was not ultimately a Western characteristic. There were distinctive features also in the classical definition of state and citizen. There were no clear boundaries to government functions – no fully articulated concepts of rights or limitations; and citizens in principle owe everything in duty to the state. These, too, did not really survive as durable Western standards.

Healthcare illustrates the difference between the Greek state and the later Western state in terms of boundaries. Greek cities routinely employed doctors to treat the sick, whether citizens or not. These doctors were more prestigious than those in private practice. In contrast, Western governments only considered this responsibility after World War II. In those countries with a state system today – and systems still vary greatly – private practice still carries greater fame. The Western state is not the classical Greek state revived.

A practice of democracy did, to be sure, develop, particularly in classical Athens. Democracy was even more widely discussed in political theory, and ordinary citizens had a voice, though limited, in the Roman republic. From this, many students are taught, in the Western civ tradition, that Western democracy has its roots in the classical past – which, of course, would also make it the oldest democratic tradition in the world, another manifestation of how Western civ can be used to sanctify. To be sure, classical democracy was different from modern: it involved direct citizen participation, not the election of representatives. And half of all males – slaves, foreigners – as well as all women had no voice. But the real problem with looking to the classical past for a solid Western democratic tradition is, first, that democracy was more the exception than the rule and, second, that the democracies that did exist were temporary, vanishing without direct trace in Western Europe later on.[1]

In more modern times, when ordinary people began to demand democracy, they never invoked Athens. There were a few cases, in Italy in the 14th and 15th centuries, when crowds harked back to the Roman republic. But elsewhere in Europe most of the first democratic stirrings invoked Christianity – the idea of all people having souls – not a classical heritage. Late 15th century

English peasants, claiming a voice, referred to the imagined equality of the Garden of Eden, not Periclean Athens. The burden of proof is on those who claim to see in the classical period a real, ongoing democratic source. There is no civilizational coherence here.

Political theorists in the Italian Renaissance (15th century) and again in the 18th century Enlightenment did discuss ancient democracy. This might provide some additional legitimacy for democratic stirrings in the Enlightenment, for thinkers such as Thomas Jefferson. But it did not cause the stirrings.

There is a Western political tradition, as we will see, though, of course, subject both to variation and change, but it owes little if anything to direct survivals from Greece and Rome except in the areas of political theory and – from Rome – law.

Much of the discontinuity between classical Greece and Rome and what became Western civilization resulted, of course, from the substantial collapse of Rome in Western Europe (though not in Eastern) by the 5th century CE. Even high culture was eclipsed, though elements here could later be revived. Social forms, however, along with popular culture and most aspects of politics changed shape as the result of Rome's fall and the impact of invasions and chaos. Even the Latin language could not hang on, influencing but not in the end fully defining the mixture of languages that became part of the Western tradition.

More than disruption was involved here. Outside Italy, the hold of Roman civilization had not penetrated too deeply. One of the several reasons Rome fell in the West was that many ordinary people had not been tightly attached – another reason to doubt too much continuity between the classical period and what became Western civilization. The fact that Spain, another Western region heavily influenced by Rome, was for several centuries ruled by Muslims, rather than participating fully in the later development of the West, further explains the gaps that opened up.

Of course there was a legacy. Either directly, or more commonly through later revival, important features of the Greco–Roman achievement did participate in Western civilization. The question is the amount of selectivity involved. There was also the sheer memory of greatness. Even Westerners who had little in common with the denizens of Greece and Rome might share some sense of the glories of Athenian culture or the grandeur of the Roman Empire. The Western civ tradition itself often builds on this memory. And the memory in turn complicates the debate about how much really survived.

3. The medieval option

The term "Middle Ages," to designate West European history from the fall of Rome until the 15th century (450–1450, approximately), is truly unfortunate. It resulted from the view of Renaissance and Enlightenment thinkers that this long period was dominated by disorder plus excessive religiosity and superstition. It implies – and many Renaissance thinkers undoubtedly believed this – that the Middle Ages disrupted the Western tradition, which was restored only when people returned to classical styles and literary themes. Instead of encouraging careful analysis of the classical connections, it tends to close the discussion before it properly begins.

Fortunately, we know a lot more than this about the Middle Ages, even though the term is still used in European history (though not, any more, in world history, where it has no applicability at all). And it is perfectly plausible to argue that the Middle Ages really should be called the foundation period of Western civilization, with due acknowledgment, first, that selective heritage from the classical period was also involved and, second, that the medieval version of Western civilization would have to change a lot before it became recognizably modern. (But on this second point: classical China and India also had to change a lot before they became recognizably modern, which does not mean that they cannot be legitimately seen as originating ongoing civilization traditions.)

The Middle Ages played a formative role in creating a definable Western civilization in two respects: first, though many changes would set in after the Middle Ages developed, there are straight-line links between a host of medieval patterns and what came later. No disruption of the magnitude of Rome's fall shatters this kind of continuity. And second – and ultimately more important – several innovations during the Middle Ages clearly established durable Western features, still discernible today.

On the first point: several centuries of confusion, including economic dislocations, highly local political institutions, low levels of intellectual life and recurrent invasions, undoubtedly describe most of Western Europe between the 5th century and the 10th centuries. Thereafter some stabilizations occurred, including considerable economic improvement and population growth. It is during these centuries of consolidation particularly that several key trends set in that can be linked directly, though amid great change, to the present.

A simple but fundamental example. By the 11th century, small central governments began to be defined in places like England and France, complete with modest bureaucracies. This set the basis for a process of political development, including periodic further expansions of state apparatus, that ultimately flows into the 20th century state. This does not mean that one could predict the 20th century state from its medieval predecessor, just that there is a continuous history.

The same applies to science. The scientific thinking and experimentation that began in the Middle Ages, in this case utilizing some revived awareness of Greek scientific achievements, plus active imitations of Arab science, launched a process that would link directly with the 17th century scientific revolution and on into the full emergence of modern science.

Again, this is not meant to argue that modern Western science became inevitable a thousand years ago, just that there is a connected historical process.

The same applies to merchants. The revival of trade in the Middle Ages generated a new merchant tradition, and from this point there is a continuous history on into more modern business activities.

The recognition of some linked historical processes would not be terribly meaningful – might, in fact, be quite misleading – if it were not also true that some of the characteristic flavor of Western civilization took shape at the same time.

It was in the Middle Ages, for example, that it became clear that Western civilization would be defined by sharp political divisions and a great deal of internal military strife. What unity there was came in the form of shared values – initially, a single version of Christianity that itself took full root during the Middle Ages – and some roughly common social and economic patterns. By the early 21st century, with the European Union, it may turn out that this long characteristic of Western civilization is being reversed, with an effective political unity and a decline of militarism. But certainly, until that point, the medieval heritage persisted with a vengeance. The West is not the only civilization with political divisions and a high degree of militarism (Japan can be compared; also subSaharan Africa), but it probably comes close to the top of the charts.

A special role for merchants also emerged in the Middle Ages, that deserves comparison with other civilization traditions. The point must be stated carefully. Several civilizations, headed by the Muslim Middle East, had more advanced merchant forms in this period, including methods and motives we would clearly designate as capitalist. Indeed, Islam was initially far friendlier to merchant activity than Christianity was. Merchant efforts did expand in medieval Western Europe, and though they were not typical a few definite capitalists emerged. What was distinctive, though, was the extent to which, given relatively weak governments, merchants managed to claim a considerable degree of autonomy as well as local political voice. Here there is some interesting contrast with Asian civilizations where trade itself was more advanced but political controls stronger, and some basis for later commercial developments within the West.

In intellectual life, the Middle Ages set up a debate about the boundaries between faith and reason that long-shaped Western discourse and that continues to reverberate at least in particularly religious parts of the West such as the United States. The depth of Christian commitment combined with the revived interest in science and logic, including some new experimentation, to produce an active cultural tension – sometimes bitter, sometimes creative. Islam experienced a similar tension – indeed, the West borrowed part of the debate from Islam – but it was in the West that the tension ultimately proved most durable.

Some medievalists have traced the origins of a distinctive Western approach to technology to the Middle Ages. The argument is not that the Middle Ages were technologically very advanced – there were important gains, but Western Europe lagged well behind Asia. Rather, the claim is that Christianity, in setting a sharp distinction between humankind and the rest of nature, encouraged an openness to technologies that would better harness (and sometimes abuse) nature for human gain. It was also, of course, true that the economic expansion of the later Middle Ages, plus the appetite for military activities, created other reasons for interest in technological advance. Europe became a particularly eager borrower of technologies – such as the printing press, the compass, and explosive power, but also the humble horse collar which allowed horses to be used for plowing, which were initially developed elsewhere.

The Middle Ages generated the idea of a limited state – not, again, in its modern forms, but in ways that link directly to the modern forms. There are two crucial points here, and their coexistence also proved critical. First, because the Christian Church in the West began without direct political support – and occasionally, during the Roman Empire, with active political opposition – it developed its own institutional structure, separate from the state. This structure and its independence solidified during the chaotic centuries of the early Middle Ages, when there simply was little state to be found. As a separate institution, claiming superiority because of its religious mission, the church often served as a check on the state, during the later Middle Ages and beyond. And even aside from its institutional role, Western Christianity encouraged the idea that religious commitments and political obligations might differ, and that the religious were more important. These patterns differed considerably both from Eastern Christianity, where the church–state relationship was more blurred, and from Islam, where the idea of the state's religious obligations took fuller root. Recurrently, in the West, religion would check the state, and this was unusual.

The second component of the West's idea of a limited state came from the evolution of Western feudalism (in interesting contrast to Japanese feudalism which was in many respects, by sheer coincidence, quite similar). This evolution began after the last serious attempt, by the Emperor Charlemagne around 800, to pretend that Roman imperial glory could ever be recaptured; the failure of the effort made it clear that some other structure would have to be used for the Western state, and feudalism, already in the works, proved to be that mechanism.

Western feudalism was a set of political relationships between lords and vassals. Vassals were supposed, among other things, to advise their lords. As certain lords became more powerful – and this included the kings of France and England as feudal lords – they often tried to cut into some of the traditional rights key vassals thought they enjoyed. Vassals often responded by developing an increasingly contractual approach to their version of feudalism:

I'll do my duties to you as lord (including military service) only if you do your duties to me (including not asking me to pay money to you beyond traditional levels and also including asking me for advice). An 11th century document by the bishop of Chartres, in France, noted that lords should act toward their vassals "reciprocally" and that if they did not, they would be "justly considered guilty of bad faith." Here was a tit-for-tat approach that encouraged careful monitoring of political leaders and also a growing array of lawyers (another Western trait) to deal with disputes. From this jostling in turn, by the 13th century came the development of formal councils that feudal vassals insisted the kings and lords call, among other things to seek approval for any new taxes. Councils of this sort cropped up in England in 1265 and also in Catalonia (Spain), France, and many central European regions. And soon they became known as parliaments.

These parliaments were not, of course, modern; the conversion to a modern Western parliament would begin only in the 17th century, and then later still some real element of democracy (quite foreign to the Middle Ages approach) entered in. It is also true that many societies with powerful regional military leaders developed a tradition of councils, to help form alliances and reduce internal strife. Council traditions emerge in Africa, in India, and elsewhere, often to help select new rulers. But the Western parliamentary tradition did have some distinctive features, particularly when combined with the unusual role of the Church. Parliaments were expected to be called reasonably regularly (though this was recurrently in dispute) and, above all, they were focused on their claimed right to approve taxation. This right, in turn – which could lead to the need to seek approval for other activities where taxes were involved – proved central to the Western parliamentary tradition (and to the American revolution, with its no taxation without representation), and remains central to the present day.

Compare, for example, the medieval Western parliament with the more common kind of conciliar tradition. The Afghan tradition of the *loya jirga*, or grand council, may go back several thousand years. According to legend, when it was time to select a king, a great council of warriors, craftsmen, and farmers was held, naming the first king the Aryan invaders had established as their invading force moved south of the Oxus river – a process culminating when an eagle appeared from the heavens and put a crown on the head of Yama, the new ruler. As in many warrior societies, councils were called recurrently, to settle intertribal disputes, but above all to select rulers. A council in 1747, held by tribal chiefs, named the king (Ahmad Shah Durrani) who first established an Afghan state. All of this is genuinely important, but equally obviously this kind of council was not what the Western parliament was all about. Because most Western kings gained the throne by inheritance, councils were not needed for naming purposes – though the tradition among earlier Germanic tribes may have foreshadowed the emphasis on feudal advice-giving. For it was finance that Western parliaments seized upon, and since monarchs frequently sought new taxation sources, this guaranteed that these institutions would influence not the choice but the conduct of many rulers. Thus the first full parliament in England, the Long Parliament in 1295, confirmed the claim that no non-feudal levy could be established by the king without parliamentary consent. By 1305 English parliaments were building on this claim to assert their authority even over church taxes, and also to receive petitions from any English subject on matters that deserved governmental attention. No other significant conciliar tradition, outside the West, moved in this direction – until other societies began to imitate Western parliaments.

Summing it up: in culture, including the cultural basis for technology, in the role of merchants, and in various aspects of politics the Middle Ages set durable bases for important characteristics of Western civilization, in precisely those parts of Europe that have proved central to Western civilization ever since. The medieval versions of Western civilization would change greatly later on, in every instance, but not to the extent of losing recognizability. Other points had to be added in subsequently. The relaxation of serfdom in the later Middle Ages was important to the subsequent development of Western social forms, but it is a stretch to see a characteristic Western society in its medieval antecedents. And, of course, the later revival of additional aspects of classical art and philosophy generated important shifts as well, though medieval thinkers themselves had begun the process of selective assimilation, particularly in the vital area of logic.

Conclusion

A coherent Western civilization can be defined by the time of the Middle Ages, emerging, with the most characteristic medieval achievements themselves, by the 11th and 12th centuries. It was not a complete version of what Western civilization would become. It was not modern. But it did provide the kind of foundation that developments associated with Islam and Arab expansion did for Middle Eastern civilization, or classical China and India for their respective traditions.

The existence of a classical preview of some features of Western civilization cannot be denied. There are objective and emotional reasons to "want" Western civilization to begin at this earlier point. The main analytical requirement is to approach the questions of Western origins explicitly, though careful assessment, rather than through glib assumptions that, for example, since it is Western it must go back as far as any civilization can claim. The whole of civilizational history has not led up to the West, only to particular slices of it. The key point is to recognize that, amid some undeniable complexity, an assessable Western civ tradition was up and running about a thousand years ago. And, in contrast to the classical legacy, much less that of the ancient river valley civilizations, this was a tradition that would, for many centuries, feed the West alone.

Note

1 There is also a pedagogical danger in the easy equation among Greece, democracy and the West. Students become so infatuated with the association that they lose a sense of the West's real history, and with it an understanding of democracy's modern emergence. Asked to say how Russia's Peter the Great did not fully Westernize Russia in 1700, intelligent freshmen not infrequently respond that he did not make Russia democratic. Right about Peter, but totally off the mark about the West in 1700. But it is an interesting mistake, reflecting cavalier generalizations too often put forward in the Western civ teaching approach.

Further reading

Martin Bernal, *Black Athena: The Afroasiatic Roots of Classical Civilization* (New Brunswick, NJ: Rutgers University Press,1987); Mary R. Lefkowitz, *Not Out of Africa: How Afrocentrism Became an Excuse to Teach Myth as History* (New Yori; BasicBooks, 1997); Robert Hahn, *Anaximander and the Architects: The Contributions of Egyptian and Greek Architectural Technologies to the Origins of Greek Philosophy* (Albany: State University of New York Press, 2001); Fernand Braudel, *The Mediterranean and the Mediterranean World in the Age of Philip II* (New York: Harper & Row, 1996); Lynn White, *Medieval Technology and Social Change* (Oxford: Oxford University Press, 1964); Peter Edwards, *Europe and the Middle Ages* (Englewood Cliffs, NJ: Prentice Hall, 1989).

Chapter 6

The West in the world

As Western civilization took shape during the Middle Ages, its position in the world gradually, though incompletely, changed as well. The Roman Empire, one of the great assemblages of power in world history – comparable, at the time, only to the Han empire in China – was a hard act to follow. Many European leaders have wished they could project the power in the world that Rome had conveyed for several centuries. How active this sentiment was as a motive for aggressive action is hard to assess. Interestingly, a similar desire to emulate Rome (and Byzantium) has been attributed to the Russian tsars as they launched a process of expansion from about 1450 onward, and again it is not easy to say how much the Roman example was window dressing, how much real impulse.

What is clear is that the Western Europe that emerged from Rome's fall was not only incapable of emulation, but at a severe disadvantage in dealing with the world around it. Around 800, Charlemagne briefly tried to develop a Roman-like empire, and received some acknowledgement from the Byzantine emperor in the process – a sign he was aware of at least a Christian wider world. But Charlemagne's effort collapsed almost immediately after his death, yielding the divided, often war-torn Europe that became a Western staple.

Both before and after Charlemagne, Western Europe was open to a variety of invasions from elsewhere. The Muslims entered France from Spain, defeated by Charlemagne's grandfather though less because of Western strength than because the Muslims had overextended their supply lines. Muslim invasions largely stopped thereafter, because Western Europe was hardly worth the trouble. But Vikings and various central European raiders continued to press in for several centuries, enhancing the disorder from which a better organized, though still divided, Western Europe would emerge. Even after the invasions stopped, Europeans were still subject to being seized as slaves to be sold to the Arab world.

Even when greater control returned, Western Europe remained visibly backward compared to its relevant neighbors. Its technology was inferior, its cities far smaller, its nobility far less polished and opulent. As Muslim travelers conveyed it, Western Europe was considerably less prepossessing than the kingdoms of subSaharan Africa, which had (in their eyes) the merit of being partially Islamic and also rich in gold. No European city could rival Constantinople, capital of the Byzantine empire, and no European royal court could come close to its Byzantine counterpart. Even as Western Europe did become wealthier, more capable of trade and more urban, its inferiority remained obvious to anyone with a basis for comparison.

And here was an anomaly. West Europeans were a warlike people, convinced also that they possessed the one true religion – disdainful of the errors of Islam, critical of the differences from Catholic practice that marked Eastern Orthodox Christianity. (Various and bloody attacks on religious heretics within Western Europe, during the Middle Ages, including periodically the Jews, made it clear that Western religion was quite intolerant at this point.) Here was a people also at least vaguely aware of their glorious Roman heritage. And yet European development lagged in many respects, as the region was hard-pressed to hold its own in trade or cultural contacts with other parts of the Mediterranean world. Muslim writers who encountered Europeans viewed them as barbarians, incapable of advanced intellectual life. "Their bodies are large, their manners harsh, their understanding dull and their tongues heavy. . . . Those of them who are farthest to the north are the most subject to stupidity, grossness and brutishness," said a 10th century Arab geographer. How could pride and intolerance on the one hand and demonstrable backwardness on the other be combined?

These points are often raised in treatments of Western civilization. They can form part of the idea of the Middle Ages as an uncomfortable interlude between periods of classical achievement and assertions of European power. They certainly form the basis for a triumphal celebration of Europe's achievement of greater aggressiveness and dynamism from the high Middle Ages onward. And these images are not totally misleading.

But the long experience of vulnerability and the even longer sense of backwardness had three durable effects that require more explicit attention. First was a long-standing feeling of fear and inadequacy, second, enhanced by Europe's own militaristic qualities, was a real anger, a desire to punish the West's enemies and to gain greater protection from them, and the third, contradictory only on the surface, was a real desire to imitate, to copy, selectively, some of the qualities that might reduce the gap between Europe and its more glittery Mediterranean neighbors.

The desire to strike back showed about as soon as the capacity developed. The first crusade, to seize the Holy Land from Islam, was called in 1091. During the ensuing period, Western crusaders, while gaining some respect for their Muslim opponents, occasionally lashed out in bloody massacres that expressed their disdain for Islam. Several subsequent crusades also took the opportunity for side trips to attack Constantinople. Efforts to reconquer Spain for Christianity began even earlier, and won gradual success until the final expulsion of a Muslim enclave in Granada in 1492. How much a vengeful though also somewhat fearful desire to retaliate motivated European policy even after this point is hard to determine, but worth considering. Here was a civilization with a definite, if understandable, chip on its collective shoulder.

The interest in imitation joined Western civilization to several other societies in the centuries after the fall of the classical empires. As civilization spread as a form of human organization to new parts of subSaharan Africa, to Japan, and to Russia, as well as to northwestern Europe, the opportunity to copy older and better-developed neighbors was a logical response. Japan, for example, imitated Chinese writing, religion and philosophy, other aspects of culture, and to a degree social forms as well. Russia copied Byzantine religion and other cultural features, as well as some political symbolism.

Western Europe, in imitating its Muslim and Byzantine neighbors, really followed the same basic process. It had less need of certain cultural fundamentals; it already had an alphabet, for example. And in imitating two neighbors, rather than just one, it may have gained a greater degree of flexibility.

But the process of imitation was both active and fruitful nevertheless. Some aspects of this have long been part of the story of Europe's Middle Ages. By the 11th and 12th centuries many scholars and translators were working in places like Muslim Toledo, in Spain, or in Constantinople, making available materials in science and philosophy. And while many of these were Greek works, many also came from Arab and Jewish sources in various parts of the Middle East and Spain. This was not simply a mastering of one aspect of the classical legacy, but a wider process of learning from advanced neighbors. And when Western scholars began debating the relationship of faith and reason they relied heavily on the example of Arab thinkers like Averroes (Ibn Rushd), though they cited them, as non-Christians, less often than they did pre-Christian examples such as Aristotle. Similarly, copying Arab medicine (itself partly derived from Greeks) was essential to launch a new medical tradition in Europe, where the direct classical legacy had vanished.

Western hunger for foreign technology has also been noted, though it deserves even further emphasis. From the Arabs or contacts with the Chinese, the West learned of the compass and the astrolabe, of superior maps, of printing, playing cards, explosive powder, and other items. It was the opportunity for more extensive imitation, as well as sheer curiosity and a taste for trade or for missionary religion, that impelled a number of West Europeans to take advantage of unprecedented opportunities to travel to central and east Asia in the 13th and 14th centuries, when the tolerant Mongol overlords controlled the region. One of the reasons Western Europeans were first in line to travel to China was their established pattern of recognizing aspects of Asian superiority and their eagerness to learn from it directly. Small wonder that in resultant travel accounts such as Marco Polo's, readers were treated to descriptions of societies whose earthly achievements far surpassed those of Europe. The new literature might spark further curiosity but it could also feed the sense of inferiority.

Eagerness for various luxury products available from foreign sources developed along with enthusiasm for new technologies. The crusades ultimately failed, but not before many European aristocrats had spent some time in the Middle East and had learned about the spices (including sugar) and other delights of upper-class material life in a richer society. The desire to maintain the supply of these items through trade became a significant economic motive in Western Europe. Contact with the Middle East and North Africa also brought knowledge of new care in cooking, which in turn helped create significant Western cuisine for the first time (starting in Italy). Delicacies such as sherbets were copied from Islam, as part of this connection. And important new foodstuffs, including new strains of wheat, were introduced to Europe as well; North African wheat, now grown in Europe, proved particularly appropriate for making pasta.

But there were other facets of imitation beyond consumer items, in a society implicitly aware that it had a long way to go by the standards of many of its neighbors. Western merchants who went to the Middle East (essential for gaining access to most Asian products) learned new business methods, including more advanced accounting and banking procedures. They also maintained the process of emulating the upper-class Muslim standard of living. When the merchant Jacques Coeur built his mansion in the French city of Bourges, in the 15th century, he carefully installed the kind of running water system he had encountered in the Middle East, along with other foreign amenities.

On a broader scale, Western architecture and structural engineering were influenced by the examples of Muslim religious buildings and particularly the towering minarets that served the daily call to prayer. Here were components of the new Gothic style – another key Western architectural form, after the classical – that serves as an emblem of medieval prosperity and the desire to honor God through soaring buildings. New ideas of etiquette also spread from contact with upper-class Muslims, on the part of returning crusaders, merchants, even former slaves and prisoners.

Some scholars have noted an influence also for Muslim law, particularly in the areas of commercial and international law. Here, too, Western Europe was able to take advantage of a better-developed legal system in precisely those areas in which it was just beginning to flex its own muscles. Legal protections for merchants as they traveled came from Islam; so, apparently, did the idea of laws governing treatment of certain categories of people, such as children or the elderly. Again, imitation could pay off, as Western Europeans came to appreciate the ethical standards which Islam had achieved. None of this reduced the official disdain for Islam as a religion, and the considerable fear of Islam as well; but it was intriguing that not just power factors or material standards, but some of the less tangible qualities of Middle-Eastern life proved so attractive.

Clearly, key European advances during the Middle Ages owed much to external example, which does not detract at all from the idea of Western achievement. Openness to ideas from the outside is not an automatic quality in human affairs, and at this point Europeans, like the Japanese, were adept at the process. This helped them a lot even if the Western civ tradition has tended to minimize, though not entirely to ignore, the imitative process, preferring to see recovery of the classical past more than copying of Islam.

What was unusual was the mixture of respect and disdain that surrounded the whole process. Japan ultimately decided not to copy some Chinese features, and, indeed, when China was invaded by the Mongols but Japan was spared, concluded that Japan had become superior to its mentor. But (except briefly in the 1590s) there was little aggressive spirit attached to this evolution, just a change in the perceived relationship by the end of the 14th century. Western Europe, in contrast, resented and even attacked the same societies it was imitating. Partly this reflected divergences within the population: scholars might copy and admire while religious leaders thundered against Islam, or while merchants hoped to gain an advantage by weakening Constantinople. But partly it was real ambivalence.

At the end of the Middle Ages European institutions had advanced in many respects. The region was no longer prey to invasion. Its appetite for wider international contacts was growing, as evidenced by a series of expeditions from the 13th century onward to seek new ways to reach Asia. But its economic lag had not been entirely cured and its sense of insecurity and resentment had not been entirely resolved. This was a volatile combination, and it would have further international impact even as Western civilization entered a new historical phase.

Further reading

Jerry Bentley, "Cross-Cultural Interaction and Periodization in World History," *The American Historical Review* **101** (1996): 749–70; Archibald Lewis, "The Islamic World and the Latin West 1350–1500," *Speculum* **65** (1990): 833–44; Manfred Wenner, "The Arab/Muslim Presence in Medieval Europe," *International Journal of Middle East Studies* **12** (1980): 59–79. For an intriguing critique of exaggerations about Western science, Dick Teresi, *Lost Discoveries: The Ancient Roots of Modern Science – from the Babylonians to the Maya* (New York: Simon & Schuster, 2002).

Part III

The rise of the West, 1450–1850

There is absolutely no question but that the West's position in the world began to change dramatically in the later 15th century, beginning with the voyages of discovery down the African coast and ultimately across the Atlantic. There is no question, either, that the nature of the West itself began to change significantly, partly because of its new position in the world. There is no question, finally, that some aspects of these shifts are extremely familiar to American students, providing some staple lessons about Western dynamism and flexibility and about connections between North America and the European heartland of Western civilization.

The chapters in this section do not intend to overturn conventional views entirely. They do seek to clarify changes, raise some questions about the causes of change, and explore new issues about extensions of Western geography that resulted from the West's success. The chapters do note that some of the familiar shifts were more gradual than has often been imagined: the "rise of the West" was not an overnight affair, and vestiges of earlier deficiencies continued for quite a while. Partly because of this, we also extend the time period usually assigned to "early modern" Europe, arguing that some key developments were not fully worked out until the middle of the 19th century. (Early modern history usually means 1450–1789.)

Many programs devoted to presenting major features of world history, but with special attention to Western history, frankly fall apart when they reach these early modern centuries. A balanced global treatment suddenly becomes entirely Western, as if nothing going on in the rest of the world mattered save, perhaps, as the West itself caused it.

The state of California, for example, offers guidelines for world history in grades six and seven. The Grade six program focuses on the early periods. It does privilege the Greeks and the Hebrews as central to the "Foundation of Western Ideas," but we have seen that this is defendable to a point. Early civilizations in India and China are framed under the rubric "West Meets East," which is misleading in implying that Asia was just pining to encounter Europe, but the substance of the unit is solid as the "west" part drops away. Grade Seven starts out well, with a reprise on the fall of Rome and then appropriate attention to the rise of Islam (qualified only by a sense that "Greek thought" alone provided any currents of rationalism within Islam, which is an error both serious and insulting). Africa, China, Japan and the Americas receive good treatments, though the Standards unfortunately insist on calling the period "the Middle Ages" regardless of the society in question. Discussion of medieval Europe is actually surprisingly brief and critical (with considerable space given to recurrent persecutions of the Jews and even nastiness to Muslims by Spanish Christians).

But then comes the Europe of Renaissance, Reformation and Scientific Revolution, and what had been the world suddenly becomes the West European subcontinent. After Europe is suitably transformed through the classical revival, Protestantism, and modern science, it then strikes out on a larger stage, particularly with the Age of Exploration and the conquest of the Americas, and finally enjoys the 18th century Enlightenment with its portentous impact on the future of Western political thought. Any warts on the Western carcass that might be seen in the Spanish "plunder and destruction of native cultures" in the Americas are more than erased by the fact that the English finally beat the Spanish in the 1588 defeat of the Armada plus the magnificent achievements of the English Bill of Rights, the French Declaration of the Rights of Man and the Citizen, and the American Declaration of Independence. And that is it for the early modern centuries: the rest of the world was either doing nothing or, perhaps, watching with awe at the procession of Western achievements and waiting for them to reach their own shores when the Europeans got around to it. Needless to say, this is not the real early modern world, or the more complicated place of Western civilization in it. Which is why even some familiar developments deserve to be briefly reviewed.

Chapter 7

Causes of a new global role

Western Europe began to show signs of new territorial energy by the 11th and 12th centuries. The Crusades were one manifestation, but while they enjoyed brief success in capturing Jerusalem they led to no durable acquisitions. More important was a push eastward by German settlers, into territories now part of eastern Germany, Poland and the Baltic States.

Even earlier, in the 10th century, Viking adventurers had crossed the Atlantic, reaching Greenland and then North America, which they called Vinland. But they encountered native Americans whose weaponry was good enough to give them pause, and they found nothing to warrant further effort – so there were no durable results. Settlements in Greenland and Iceland, however, persisted. Most Viking energy, not devoted to raids in Western Europe, actually went into contributing to a trade route through western Russia to Constantinople, and so bypassed "Western civilization."

As early as 1291 two Italian brothers, the Vivaldis from Genoa, sailed with two galleys through the Straits of Gibraltar, seeking a Western route to the "Indies," the spice-producing areas of south and southeast Asia. They were never heard from again. Early in the 14th century, other Genoese explorers rediscovered the Canary Islands, in the South Atlantic, populated by a hunting-and-gathering people. Vaguely known since classical times, the islands had not been contacted by Europeans. Genoese sailors also visited the Madeiras and probably reached the more distant Azores by 1351. Soon after this, Spanish ships began sailing along the African coast as far south as present-day Sierra Leone. All this occurred, however, when the main Afro–Eurasian trade routes were dominated by Middle Eastern traders. Prior to the 1430s, the big new development in these trade patterns involved the great voyages of the Chinese, through the Indian Ocean all the way to Africa; only when these were canceled, in an imperial policy decision, did the European flutterings begin to play a more substantial role.

During the 15th century, voyages sponsored by the Portuguese monarch Henry "the Navigator" pushed further and further down the African coast, seeking access to Asia. The series was finally crowned in triumph in 1498, when Vasco da Gama made it around the Cape of Good Hope and reached

India. Combined with Columbus's trips to the Americas, from 1492 onward, the European push into growing world trade influence was in full swing.

The initial trips were costly, at a time when Europe was poor. They sought wealth, but initially they produced little. They were also extremely dangerous, as the Vivaldis' probable fate demonstrates. Sailing into literally uncharted waters, at a time when most Europeans believed the world was flat, the expeditions required great courage.

And the question is, what motivated them? How can they best be explained?

Two elements of the context are obvious, in commerce and religion, though no less important as a result. And one possible cause is strangely missing. The voyages occurred as part of Europe's commercial growth. Heavy Italian involvement followed from the role of Italian merchants in dealing with Asian goods in the Mediterranean and from their strong profit motives and considerable business sophistication. Portuguese and Spanish involvement followed partly from geography, in terms of a peninsula extending into the Atlantic, but also from strong Christian motivations at a time when the Muslim expulsion was just being completed and momentum tended to carry Iberian rulers into further adventures. How much a specifically Christian missionary zeal was involved – early explorers tended to claim their Christian duty more than doing much about it – is unclear, but a more general religious push was almost certainly involved.

Many individual adventurers, like most of the Spanish conquerors in Latin America, had been blocked at home. They sought profit above all – whether related to the larger merchant tradition, or simply reflecting personal hunger – and their Christianity consisted principally of believing that they could treat non-Christians any way they chose, a heritage of the long European struggle against Jews and Muslims. But these intense personal motivations do not mean that larger causes, including ultimately a genuine missionary zeal, were not involved.

The European surge did not, however, reflect population pressure (in contrast to earlier developments such as the extension of Germanic settlements eastward toward Poland). This would normally be high on the list of possibilities, but does not apply here. Hit by bubonic plague, the European population was actually declining during the first exploration period – which makes the issue of causation all the more interesting.

So why did Europeans venture out in such new, dramatic and ultimately highly consequential ways?

Here is the conventional explanation, beyond the selective elements from the medieval context. Western Europe was changing rapidly. In particular, a new spirit was developing in Renaissance Italy. This spirit was secular, touting achievement here on earth. It saw no limits to human endeavor. A leading modern Europe textbook of the early 1970s, by Eugen Weber, a really good if Western-enthusiastic historian, sees this spirit leading to new inventions, to a "towering imagination," to a new sense of "liveliness, originality, and vividness", as evident in the overall mentality as in the new styles in art and music. This was a spirit that would easily spill over into business and, of course, into exploration, aided only by a few other props like better maps.

So, a new dynamism in Western culture, soon to become characteristic, comes first, and the explorations (carefully placed, in Weber's account, in the following chapter, to make the implicit but solid casual connection quite clear) follow as result.

It is, of course, true that the explorers were brave if not foolhardy, and that a disproportionate number came from Italy. But why did their ventures start before the Renaissance took hold? Why did they center in Spain and Portugal that were not at the time, and indeed never became, real bastions of the Renaissance spirit?

A more recent edition of an even more successful textbook, the great work of R. R. Palmer, again a very fine historian indeed, offers a slightly more diffuse approach while shying away from explicitly discussing causation. Palmer and his colleagues, in their ninth edition, do note Europe's inferiority in technology to Asia, but in a short paragraph easily bypassed. More obviously, they still precede their discussion of the explorations with a long chapter on changes within Europe through the 16th century (well after, obviously, the pattern of explorations had been launched). In this launching chapter they not only emphasize, along with the Protestant Reformation, the Renaissance – again, though without quite so much hyperbole about its confident, individualistic spirit – but also the new political styles emerging with the "New Monarchs" on the 16th century, who claimed more substantial powers than their medieval predecessors had done. The clear implication is that Western strength, now heightened by new, postmedieval ingredients, is all one needs to consider. The West, or at least the increasingly modern West, equals growing dynamism equals a growing place in the world at large.

But two problems, apart from the complexities in chronology and geography. In the first place, the whole exploratory surge depended on important new technologies: as another historian, Carlo Cipolla, puts it, on "guns, sails" and navigational devices. During the two centuries after 1492, European power went where ships and ships' cannon could take it and, with the important exception of the Americas, not beyond. The Europeans increasingly grabbed select ports and islands in Africa and Asia, where the naval technology was crucial, and they dominated most ocean-going trade, even where European goods and markets were not directly involved. But they could not normally move inland in Africa and Asia. The Americas were an exception because of the larger technological disjuncture, against peoples who were not using metals, who had no horses and who, additionally, were quickly decimated by imported diseases.

Where did the crucial new technologies come from? Not, it should be stressed, from some new European technological genius or a new worldly spirit. Rather, the basis for naval advance came from growing knowledge of Arab and Chinese technologies. The compass was imported directly. New sailing ship designs built on Arab advances, though additional innovations were essential. The acquisition of explosive powder was, of course, crucial, coming from China possibly via Arab intermediaries. Here, too, the Europeans added on to the imported technology. Skilled in large metal casting thanks to the experience of manufacturing huge church bells – in one of those odd coincidences of history: no one had planned church bells with the idea of later military applications in mind – and operating in a warlike society, Europeans by the 14th century were introducing guns and canons, made both from bronze and from iron. Explosions could now be guided and projected better than the Chinese had managed.

Again, it is hard to find any special Renaissance spirit here, particularly given the early timing of the major imitations. It does take skill and flexibility to import new technologies. Many societies would turn away from guns and gunpowder because of cultural aversion to such stark technological innovation or because of concern for the impact on an established social structure that depended on older, pre-gun methods of fighting. This latter social concern, aimed at protecting the position of the feudal samurai, ultimately pulled Japan away from an interest in imitating European gun technology. But recognizing Europe's particular agility in appropriating an essentially borrowed technology hardly echoes the textbook hymns to an individualistic, tradition-shedding Renaissance culture.

And there is more. While strong profit-making and military motives clearly entered into the age of exploration, the surge was also predicated on some long-standing European weaknesses that were, if anything, getting worse. Along with technological imitation, the real jump start for Europe's rise came from an effort at problem-solving more than from tapping some special culture of enterprise or individualism.

Issue number one was what, today, we would call a severe balance of payments deficit. Elite Europeans delighted in luxury products from Asia, from spices to silks. The trade was not high volume, but it was costly. Europe had relatively little to offer in return. The West's manufacturing was not up to Asian standards, particularly in the realm of quality products. There were no special foods or resources of interest. Seizure of Europeans as slaves remained possible, but there was no organized traffic as developed in East Africa, to service the Middle East. Precious metals were the only extensive means of payment open to Europeans, but the subcontinent had no significant holdings of gold, and only modest resources in silver.

When Vasco da Gama reached India in 1498, he brought some crude iron pots and cloth – the fruits of European manufacture at that point. The Muslim merchants who dominated trade on India's western coast were not happy at the sight of potential competitors in any event, but they particularly scorned goods for which they had absolutely no use. Had da Gama not brought some gold, he would have been unable to purchase the Indian spices that he in fact took home to use to demonstrate the potential importance of a regular Portuguese-Indian trade connection. Here, in a nutshell, was a serious problem: what to offer, on a regular basis, for these highly lucrative Asian goods.

And this, in turn, in addition to simple greed and a great deal of credulousness about native wealth just around the corner, helps explain why Europeans, in probing Africa and soon Latin America, were so hungry for gold, so eager to believe that massive treasures awaited discovery. When gold did not materialize, Europeans often turned to what, in modern times, we would call import substitution. They began producing sugar, first in places like the Canary Islands and the Madeiras, to reduce their need to bring it from Asia. When they lacked local labor to raise sugar, often because of the impact of the diseases they unwittingly but devastatingly imported – first in the Atlantic islands, then in the Americas – they turned to the seizure of slaves in West Africa. While nothing in modern eyes can justify this recourse, the deep economic problem the Europeans faced helps explain why they were so ready to light on any option.

The second problem the Europeans faced, and tried to solve through the expeditions, involved their distaste at relying on Muslim merchants for these highly valued goods. This was partly an economic, partly a religious issue. While various Mediterranean European merchants profited handsomely from their dealings with Muslims, and while Europeans increasingly outdid the Muslims in the Mediterranean proper, it was true that, fundamentally, the Muslims held the upper hand. They were the ones who obtained the precious goods from the rest of Asia, bringing them to ports in Egypt or the Middle East where the Europeans would arrive to bargain. The added costs of these transactions simply worsened the balance of payments problem. But there was also the religious conundrum, of depending so heavily on merchants of a heretical faith.

Tensions with Islam worsened with the failure and ultimate ending of the crusades. While Islamic political power suffered a reverse with the collapse of the strongest Arab political unit, the caliphate, in 1261, along with powerful Mongol invasions, the Middle Eastern economy was in fact rebounding within a century – exactly the point at which European zeal for exploration began to intensify. Trade in the Indian Ocean was increasing from 1398 onward through a new, Muslim spice export center established in Malacca in present-day Indonesia. Finally, by this point a new Muslim imperial power, not Arab but Turk, was taking shape as well. In 1453 it conquered the Christian bastion of Constantinople, and while Western Christians had ignored Byzantine pleas for aid, the shock of this power shift reverberated widely. It was not implausible to think of Islam as again on the march, and this inevitably encouraged efforts to loosen their stranglehold on Asian trade. One sign of the new tension was the closing off of European interest in imitating developments in the Islamic world (a narrowness that was reciprocated by Muslims, who long ignored European advances). (We will see in the next chapter that one bit of intellectual imitation may have persisted at least to the 15th–16th century, but it was not acknowledged.)

(The West's new aversion to imitating Middle Eastern civilization did not apply to new consumer items such as tulips or later carpets. By the 17th century Europeans began to import the new Arab passion for coffee and coffee houses, which also, for a while, were male dominated like their Middle Eastern progenitors.)

The European trade situation contrasted obviously with that of established powers such as China. China depended on some imports, for example for certain prized types of tea, but it had no problem paying for them with manufactured goods, including not only silks, but also porcelains. There was even a contrast with subSaharan Africa. This region, like Europe, had long been an imitator. It traded actively with North Africa and the Middle East but at an obvious disadvantage. But the fact was, first, that there were plenty of goods to exchange, in the form of salt, gold, slaves, and other commodities. No fundamental bargain of payments deficit emerged. And second, Africans, many of whose leaders were Muslim, felt no discomfort in dealing with Arab Islam; there was no need to resent a religious–economic dependence.

The result, of course, was that Europe was moved to venture out in new ways, and this did both demonstrate and produce new dynamism – in contrast, for example, to the more settled patterns of Africa that additionally lacked a seafaring tradition. But the extent of European dependence, the extent to which they operated from weakness rather than a soaring sense of new strength, would long mark the Western surge.

When da Gama took his second expedition to India, in 1502, he had no new goods to offer. But this time he brought a fighting fleet of 21 vessels, bent on overpowering the Muslim merchants and forcing access to further trade. Coming from a country long accustomed to bitter battles with Muslims at home, Da Gama and his troops had no compunctions about a variety of physical atrocities. Cities and ships were burned, prisoners butchered and dismembered, with body parts taken home as trophies – or sent to other parts of India as symbols of the arrival of a new power. But the tone reflected religious tension, even a sense of embattled inferiority, not the proud bearers of a more confident Western culture.

The same odd combination between growing naval strength and continued uncertainty showed in the reactions of European explorers to many of the new places they began to visit. Columbus, to be sure, wrote scathingly of the "natives" he encountered in the Caribbean, with their lack of clothing and weaponry. But people who saw the Aztec cities in Mexico were full of praise for their splendor, to which European cities were often unfavorably compared. The same held in Africa, where Europeans often noted the magnificence of royal courts. In the same context, European missionaries sent to India and China often went native, not losing their Christianity but becoming immersed in the local culture. Sometimes this was a ploy to help win local favor for what was really important, the religion; but often it recognized the strength of the Asian patterns of dress, manners and overall standards of living. But even as this admiration surfaced, Europeans (not always the same ones, but sometimes) showed no compunction in attacking and, in the case of Africans, enslaving. Advantages in military technology and a sense of need could authorize cruel exploitation – and the sense that some of the people involved had superior accomplishments might make the process worse.

With time, of course, Europeans gained further ground. By the 17th century European wealth was beginning to expand rapidly, though there were many desperately, perhaps increasingly, poor wage earners as well. While there was no technological revolution, the opportunity to sell abroad plus growing wealth at home helped spur innovations in metallurgy and, soon, in textiles. Europe was no longer technologically inferior to Asia overall, and the latter's pace of change was unquestionably challenged. Finally, the quality of European craft products improved also, for example in furnishings, making them desirable commodities in some overseas markets such as the homes of American planters or, soon, Russian noblemen.

But a balance of payments issue persisted, nevertheless, for European taste for Asian goods showed no sign of slowing down. It was in the 17th century that the appetite for Chinese porcelain became so overwhelming that the product became known, in English, simply as china. The problem of how to pay for the goods was changed by Europe's growing good fortune, but it did not disappear.

Which is why, as world historians have recently been emphasizing, the nation that ended up importing more New World silver than any other was – not Spain, the colonial overlord, or France or England with their superior banks – but China. Though far less aggressive and commercially oriented than the West, China, and even India, continued to enjoy a manufacturing superiority particularly in key crafts, and they won disproportionate colonial profits in consequence, without having any colonies. Europeans brought American silver to them, to Macao in China itself or to the Philippines, where it was picked up by Chinese traders, in return for the treasured Asian goods. With colonial silver in hand, the balance of payments problems pressed the Europeans far less acutely than before the decades of exploration, but they were still there – and they lasted, with regard to China particularly, into the 19th century.

In a sense, this is absolutely unsurprising. It takes a long time for power balances to shift completely, and the passing of over three centuries for Europe to shift from inferiority to overwhelming superiority may be regarded as surprisingly swift. But the whole process has been obscured by the Western-centered assumption that, as soon as the West got going, as soon as

Renaissance individualism began to radiate its dazzling charm, everyone else was left in the dust, burdened by tradition, isolation, and progressive decline. It did not work that way, and our image of the West needs to be modified, not necessarily overturned but adjusted to a more complicated early modern history, in consequence.

And, of course, the product that finally did the trick, where more fully opening trade with China was concerned, was not European at all, but a poppyseed derivative backed once again by superior European naval power.

Here, we get into relatively familiar territory, in contrast to China's lion's share of American silver. It is well known that, at the end of the 18th century, a British envoy to China, carefully required to acknowledge the majesty of the Chinese emperor, was treated to a vigorous diatribe about China's complete lack of need for anything the Western barbarians had to offer. Then, 40-plus years later, in 1839, the English converted Chinese resistance to their importation of India-grown opium into an occasion to use military force to require acceptance, opening Chinese markets for the first time in the process. Opium was more than a symbolic issue, for it really was the first good the English discovered that some Chinese could be made to want that depended on European merchants for its provision. In consequence, opium proved to be the single most valuable product in world trade through the 19th century.

Again, this is an often-told story, and certainly no credit to Western values. But concerning the China side it is usually interpreted as a consequence of centuries of stubborn, traditionalist isolation, which only a dramatic show of force could alter. In fact, the real story was how vigorous Chinese economic capacity remained, even after centuries of Western gains: only military coercion and drugs finally turned the tide.

So the complexity of the factors behind Europe's ventures into the wider world involves more than a tedious quest for accuracy in causation. The complexity really helps explain the nature as well as the motives for European initiatives, and the varied causes paint an enduring portrait as well, with consequences lasting well into the 19th century. With all this, the possibility of some input from a new, more confident Western culture remains – though there is a serious chicken-and-egg problem, particularly outside Italy, about whether new cultural and political patterns preceded, or resulted from, the first fruits of a growing role in world trade.

For even before European dominance over the balance of trade was fully acquired, by about 1850, there is no question that the European outlook toward the world was reshaped by success far earlier. Imitation largely stopped, as we have seen – though not, of course, a deep thirst for many specialty products from the four corners of the world. Awe at splendid cities and courts began to recede as well. Individual Westerners have always been able to resonate to the achievements of other cultures, but the general theme of amazement declined. To be sure, in the 18th-century Enlightenment the idea of a "noble savage" arose. Innocent primitives, such as native Americans, were depicted as having all sorts of virtues that jaded civilized people in Europe had lost. But this was a rhetorical device, not a real judgment of other places, and its patronizing qualities easily overmatched its praise-in-principle.

One of the key sources of growing condescension now involved technology. As Europeans began to become surer of their own prowess here, they translated technology into a basis for judging other civilizations and finding them wanting. This applied not just to the Americas, where the gap was huge, but even to China, as a way to feel good about a long-daunting contrast. It was around 1700 that a Jesuit missionary lamented that the Chinese could not be persuaded "to make use of new instruments and leave their old ones without an especial order from the Emperor to that effect. They are more fond of the most defective piece of antiquity than of the most perfect of the modern, differing much from us [Europeans] who are in love with nothing but what is new." Not only the position of the West in the world, but its attitude was changing, in ways we can still recognize today. A sense of superiority and the relevance of technology as a measure of society became durable additions to the meaning of Western civilization, even before the West had fully closed its gaps with Asia.

Some world historians have tried to compare the nature of growing Western supremacy with the one civilization that had previously claimed something like dominance – albeit in Afro–Eurasia rather than the whole globe: the Islamic Middle East. As West-bashers, they have argued that the West was far less tolerant than Muslims, more consistently cruel to non-believers, more bent on changing conquered peoples to its own cultural and legal norms. They have also seen the West as more thoroughly exploitative, self-righteously justified in exacting every possible profit from a subordinated region. The harsher qualities of the Atlantic slave trade and American slavery, compared to slave patterns in the Middle East, might illustrate these claims.

In fact, the judgments are difficult. Muslims could and did exploit. Greed, more than religion, is now seen as the leading motive in Arab conquests in the Middle East and North Africa in the 7th and 8th centuries. Westerners could long be fairly tolerant of other ways, as the British were in India during the 18th century even as they found ever-greater ways to profit from the region's economy. Comparative issues remain intriguing, as is the assessment of the West's use of growing world power when compared to some of the more flattering self-assessments, or the recognition of simple omissions that is common in the rosiest interpretations of Western civ.

It is true, however, that the rise of the West owed much to severe economic problems, which, in turn, generated some durable characteristics to the Western approach to world trade and to colonization. The need to overcome past inferiorities could be a powerful goad, and it imposed its own blinders on Western standards. It is also true that raw technology ruled much of the rise of the West and came to ride high in Western self-assessment. Westerners might seek to mask their growing enjoyment of world power by sincerely praising the civilized qualities of the Renaissance, and the new culture was undeniably important. But the culture's range should not be exaggerated, given the other, more basic factors in play. And it was certainly not what most of the rest of the world would see in their new encounters with Western civilization.

Further reading

R. R. Palmer, Joel Colton, and Lloyd Kramer, *A History of the Modern World*, 9th edn (New York: Knopf, 2002); Eugen Weber, *A Modern History of Europe: Men, Cultures, and Societies from the Renaissance to the Present* (New York: Norton, 1971); on Western technology, Carlo M. Cipolla, *Guns, Sails and Empires: Technological Innovation and the Early Phases of European Expansion 1400–1700* (Manhattan, Kan.: Sunflower University Press, 1965); Michael Adas, *Machines as the Measure of Men: Science, Technology and Ideologies of Western Dominance* (Ithaca: Cornell University Press, 1989); Archibald Lewis, "The Islamic World and the Latin West, 1350–1500," *Speculum* **65** (1990): 833–44; Janet L. Abu-Lughod, *Before European Hegemony: the World System, A.D. 1250–1350* (New York: Oxford University Press, 1989); Immanuel Wallerstein, *The Capitalist World-Economy: Essays* (Cambridge [Eng.]; New York: Cambridge University Press, 1979); Andre Gunder-Frank, *Reorient: Global Economy in the Asian Age* (Berkeley: University of California Press, 1998).

Chapter 8

Transformations of the West

The early modern centuries – 1450 or so well into the 18th century – are always seen as times of great change in Western Europe. Indeed, the magnitude of change is what often overwhelms textbook treatments, leading them to forget the rest of the world. This chapter, interpreting some familiar stuff, seeks to add three main points: first, to help see the woods as well as the trees. The details of the various specific change points often obscure a sense of the main transformations that were occurring. Relatedly, it is easy to lose sight of what was Western in the whole process, for this must involve connections with, as well as departures from, the earlier, formative period in the civilization. Second, as part of the big changes emphasis, it is in the early modern period that we can begin clearly to add social features to the political and cultural definitions of the West – finding some coherences that help integrate the newer kind of history with the more familiar Western civ staples and arguing that sound history and a more sophisticated version of Western civ need not be at odds. Third, we need to ask what all these transformations, accelerating from the mid-17th century onward, did to the West in the world – including how Westerners looked at the rest of the world, as well as how the world would see the West. There is no question that the West was changing faster than most societies at this point, but this does not mean that we should abandon all comparative sense to watch in wonder as the West shed an older skin for a new one.

Conventional surveys of the early modern West legitimately offer up a wide variety of specific movements, each with special names, each held by Western civ partisans to be essential knowledge for the educated man or woman. And, indeed, the sequence is fascinatingly complex.

The Italian Renaissance seemingly began the process. Mainly an elite cultural movement, one can also discuss Renaissance politics and, to a degree, trade. A key cultural complexity involves the oscillation between brave invocations of innovation and individualism and a sometimes slavish imitation of classical Roman themes and styles.

After 1450 the Renaissance moved to more northern Europe. The Northern Renaissance had many of the same features as the Italian but it was more religious, and the political changes were less stark because of the persistence of feudal monarchies. The Northern Renaissance lasted until the late 16th century and beyond, embracing such great national writers as Shakespeare and Cervantes.

As the Northern Renaissance continued, Europe was gripped by the Protestant Reformation and Catholic Reformation, in the 16th century. While some Renaissance ideas were used, aspects of the Reformation were rebellions against Renaissance secularism and humanism. The Reformation generated fierce religious controversies and many wars, and the unity of Western Christianity was never restored.

Simultaneously, and here definitely in response to the new role in overseas commerce and the silver coming in from the Americas, Europe experienced rapid commercial growth and a price revolution that, on the whole, further encouraged trade. Seemingly contradictory to Reformation religiosity, in fact some Reformation thinkers provided new justifications for trade and even saw wealth as a sign of divine favor. So there were some linkages around economic change, though some undeniable tensions as well.

Moving to the 17th century, the headline developments were the Scientific Revolution and absolutism. The Scientific Revolution built on medieval science (and through this on Arab science as well) and on Renaissance interest in secular subjects, though it really differed from the Renaissance focus on the arts and literature. New discoveries, particularly about planetary motion, led to sweeping assertions of scientific method and world view. Soon, the impact spilled over into political theory and the beginnings of social science inquiry.

Absolutism was a largely separate development in the political sphere, though some monarchs patronized scientific work. Absolutism featured a pronounced surge in claims for royal power and an expansion and rationalization of state functions, including bureaucratic growth and specialization.

Absolutism did not win over most political theorists, however. And both Britain and Holland developed parliamentary monarchies that operated rather differently, with weaker central governments and more legislative checks on royal power. This alternative pattern obviously complicated 17th century politics.

In the 18th century the main news is the Enlightenment. This was largely a cultural movement, emphasizing rationalism and political and economic theory, and it clearly built on the Scientific Revolution. Enlightenment thought had some political implications, as certain monarchs claimed to be enlightened stewards of public welfare and so modified at least the rhetoric surrounding absolutism. A new spurt of interest in human emotions and the origins of the modern novel add to the complexity of the 18th century, for on the surface at least they ran counter to Enlightenment themes. The first appearance of modern Western consumerism touched base with both the Enlightenment (which praised material progress) and this early Romanticism (which could support emotional satisfactions in the acquisition of new things).

Several points leap out from this admittedly brief summary. First, there were lots of zigs and zags in early modern Europe. There is no straight line from Renaissance to Enlightenment, particularly since intense Reformation religious passions intervene. Political themes are also complicated, and different parts of Western Europe opted for quite different combinations. Second, not all facets of Western society changed equally. After the tremendous late medieval changes in weaponry and naval patterns, technology tended to evolve more than revolutionize during the early modern period overall. There were gains, and as we have seen Europe made headway in manufacturing compared to other leading areas. The introduction of the improved printing press in 1450 was a huge innovation. But significant agricultural change, which was essential to a real restructuring of the economy given the masses of people and resources involved in what was still a largely rural economy, did not begin until the late 17th century. Then, new techniques of land reclamation, launched in Holland, combined with use of new foods and some new methods to begin more serious shifts. The pace of innovation in manufacturing also speeded up from the early 18th century onward. It was at this time, also, that rapid population gains began. But none of this characterized the early modern period as a whole, where the emphasis lay more on culture, politics, and trade. Finally, perhaps self-evidently, lots of tradition and continuity persisted even amid change. Urban people were on the whole more affected than rural. Aristocratic power continued to prevail in most parts of Europe, and even with commercial advance many business people were content with second rank status or imitated aristocratic patterns as eagerly as they could. Remnants of feudalism persisted in the political arena as well, even under absolutism which tended to claim more than it achieved. Finally, patterns of change were spotty and inconsistent. Shifts in one area – for example a growth in manufacturing and commerce – might be conditioned by a highly traditional economic focus just 20 miles away.

But there was real change, and it unquestionably accelerated from about the middle of the 17th century onward. Without belittling the conventional approach, which involves exploring one new pattern after another (despite the fact that they often confusingly overlapped), it is both possible and desirable to offer a more focused presentation. The approach admittedly reduces some of the detail and the zigzag qualities of change, but it also helps us see the ways in which Western Europe had become a rather unusual kind of agricultural civilization by the 18th century. The approach also helps clarify the relationships among categories of change, including some social currents, launched among ordinary people, that are too often downplayed or ignored. And this overview, in turn, is essential to allow us to return to the issue of Westernness, which also risks getting lost in the one-thing-after-another descriptive brew.

Historian–sociologist Charles Tilly, dealing with early modern Europe, has urged a "big changes" approach. Indeed, to dramatize his insistence on looking at major shifts, he called one of his books *Big Changes, Large Processes, Huge Comparisons*. The title is a bit awkward, but it certainly conveys a different take on the same Western Europe that usually moves, crabwise, from Renaissance onward. And Tilly sees two changes as particularly decisive in creating a new kind of Europe, increasingly separate from its past as it forged a framework which, in most respects, continues to operate. Putting the same point another way: the big changes approach shows how 18th century Europe had fundamentally shifted away from its characteristics of just two centuries before. In fact, in my judgment, Tilly's choice of two factors is a bit limited, for two others are essential as well. But this is not a massive list even so, and it provides a different kind of guide to what is arguably the most complicated chronological slice of Western history to date.

The first change, and in many ways the most obvious, involves increasing commercialization. Both domestically and around the world, European merchants played a growing role. The surge of trade had begun during the Middle Ages, was set back a bit by the dislocations of the 14th century plague, but then resumed. Renaissance values supported trade and certainly depended on it for the prosperity that could support a more elaborate culture. The Reformation, as we have seen, somewhat unwittingly might encourage business life as well, as a sign of God's favor and, sometimes, a way for a religious minority to make its mark despite discrimination in public life. But trade had larger ramifications. Many peasants began to produce more for sale on the market, rather than for purely local needs. Whole regions began to specialize in particularly advantageous crops. It was in the 17th century, for example, that southern France really began to develop a focus on wine-growing for sales around the country and beyond. In turn, other necessary foods were often imported, and other regions, less favorable to vineyards, cut back their wine-growing efforts in favor of purchasing from the market. Large numbers of rural and urban people also began to do manufacturing work at home, again for wide sales. Whole villages in Germany and France specialized in shoe production or the manufacture of small metal items such as scissors or nails. The workers involved owned their tools, but they usually received raw materials and orders from an urban capitalist, who then collected the finished products for market. Needless to say, the use of money increased in many sectors of Western society. And all of this occurred in the wider context of Europe's growing international commercial role. Merchants and government leaders alike learned that there were more profits to be had in selling and manufacturing goods, than in committing to a traditional array of products for local subsistence. Europe was pushing the conventional envelope for agricultural societies, and commercial forms and motives were the key motor of change.

Europe was hardly the only commercialized agricultural society around. Commerce was also growing in Japan, in terms of internal trade, and market agriculture also surged forward. But there were two ramifications of Europe's commercialization that added further distinctiveness.

First, social relationships were affected by growing commercialization. Merchants clearly expanded in range and number. The rise of the merchant class was complicated by the continued social and political dominance of the aristocracy. Tensions here were not fully sorted out until the age of revolution at the end of the 18th century and even beyond, when aristocratic power began to recede and merchant voices and values gained greater latitude. But the groundwork for these shifts was being laid earlier. More broadly, a new social division began to separate people who owned property – rural farmers as well as merchants, master craftsmen, and landlords – from those who largely depended on sale of their labor for a wage. Here was a major distinction from the key basis for medieval social arrangements, which had hinged largely on serf–lord relationships, and here also was the germ of the social system that still describes Western society today. For several centuries, the new division was compounded by differences in economic fortunes. Wage laborers often suffered considerable, even growing poverty, while on the whole the living standards of the property owners improved from the late 16th century onward. Associated with the division was a new attitude toward poverty, along with important remnants of older, charitable views. Many people began to argue that considerable poverty was the fault of the poor, the result of drink or laziness or some other defect, and that therefore there was no particular social responsibility to alleviate it. Here again was a consequence of commercialization whose echoes linger today, in thoughts about the faults of local poor people or the poor people in other parts of the world. The birth of a commercial society in Europe went well beyond the rise of trade.

Second, European commercialism continued to push out into new areas, as developments in the 18th century amply demonstrated. On the world stage, Europeans began to use policies, such as tariffs, to promote their own manufacturing and discourage it elsewhere. As England gained greater power in India, it limited the import of Indian cotton cloth in favor of developing a new industry at home. By the end of the 18th century tens of thousands of Indians were losing their traditional manufacturing jobs because of competition from English-made cotton cloth. This was a story that would be repeated in other parts of the world in decades to come, as European commerce claimed wider stakes. During the 18th century onward, again particularly in England, grain imports increased, from places such as Poland where rural conditions were bad and labor cheap. The bargain between commercial activity and agriculture was tipping increasingly toward the former, in key sectors of Western society, and again this process would continue. It was commercial expansion also that helped set up the first signs of modern consumerism in the 18th century in many parts of Western

Europe. Shops increased in number, and shopkeepers innovated in tactics. Advertisements sought to induce people to buy new goods. Styles changed often, and people were urged to keep up with novel fashions in clothing and furniture. Shops offered loss leaders, products on sale that would lose money in themselves, but would bring in customers who would be enticed to buy other goods. Commercial innovation was not the only cause of the signs of mass consumerism. Social change pushed people to seek new acquisitions as a sign of success and personal identity. But the combination was potent, and again commercialization pushed the West toward new frontiers.

The next big change area involved politics. Remnants of feudalism persisted, into the 18th century, but on balance the powers of the central state increased, with new bureaucracy to match, while hints of the formulation of the nation-state emerged as well. By the 18th century the characteristic European state was a new product, by Western precedent, and the forces for further change were in place as well.

The enhancement of the central state involved sending more representatives of the government to outlying areas, plus introducing a more specialized bureaucracy. Slowly, formal training of certain officials increased, in areas such as civil engineering for roads and forts, and for military posts involving new techniques such as the artillery. Governments began to take on new roles in the economy and even, haltingly, in setting some (low) standards for handling the poor. Prisons were introduced, the first time Western governments were capable of this kind of management of criminals as opposed simply to administering harsh physical punishments. There were steps toward provision of police forces. Much of this state development involved attempts to rationalize operations, to think them through in more systematic ways. For armies, European states introduced uniforms and more consistent officer grades. They provided supply services, so armies would not simply live off the land; they even set up military hospitals and some pension programs. Western capacity at deliberate organization increased.

Partly because of the growth of central states in countries such as France, it began to make a real difference what nation one lived in. A historian–anthropologist has studied a village that straddled the French–Spanish border. In the 16th century, it mattered little which side of the border a person lived on. People moved freely back and forth, and their loyalty to the village was primary. But by the 17th century distinctions between French and Spanish began to grow. Border guards made crossing more difficult. There were different laws and economic regulations. With changes of this sort, in areas that had nationwide governments like France, England, and Spain, the idea of a nation-state began to emerge. Here, the notion was that cultural identity and political boundaries should roughly coincide, with strengthened loyalties to match. This was not yet, until the end of the 18th century, full-blown modern nationalism, but it did offer a distinctive definition of the state and its relationship to popular culture. Governments such as France began to try to regulate and standardize the language, as one expression of this new equation. The French King set up a new academy to do this, and the Académie Française still tries to defend pure French today. English people began to talk more explicitly about being English, and about having certain rights because they were English. But Western civilization was not yet fully organized into nation-states: Germany and Italy were divided into smaller units, while the giant Habsburg monarchy was what would later be called "multinational." But a core of nation-states was beginning to emerge.

The third big change was quite different from politics and even commerce, because it stemmed from ordinary people. From the late Middle Ages onward, more and more Western Europeans began to develop a distinctive kind of family structure – which historians have simply dubbed, the European-style family. The structure had three features. First, it involved relatively late marriage for ordinary folk – 25 or 26 for women – a bit older for men. Second, because of this, it involved strong emphasis on the nuclear family, husband and wife and their children; extended family ties to other relatives existed, but they were weaker than elsewhere partly because marriage did not usually take place until the parents of bride and groom were elderly or even dead. And, finally, a large minority of people did not marry at all (and they were discouraged from having sex outside marriage). The basic purpose of this system seems to have been to limit the number of children per family in order to protect access to property.

The European-style family had consequences, however, beyond population controls. It created greater equality in the economic roles of husbands and wives, simply because there were few other adults in the household to help. Gender relations were still formally patriarchal, with men in charge. Many countries saw women lose access to certain skilled crafts, and in some they could not normally own property. But within this framework, women's work in the family was unusually vital. This could create some informal sharing of decision making or it could create tensions, with women asserting claims that the patriarchal system resisted. One historian has argued that wife-beating went up in consequence. Whatever the case, there was a new spark in gender relations that was less obvious in many other societies.

The result showed in the Protestant Reformation. In some ways, the Reformation ended up bolstering male authority; fathers were seen as responsible for the moral conduct and religious training of their families. But the Reformation also provided new praise for marriage, now that the clergy were encouraged to marry and monasteries were abolished. Not surprisingly, by the 17th century, Protestant writers began to comment on the need for love between men and women in a good marriage and on the importance of happiness for both parties. Again, this could produce new tensions, with women seeing the opportunity to assert new claims for political attention – this happened in England – but being turned back by authorities who argued women had no public role and should simply do what their husbands told them. The point was that gender relations in the West had been ruffled, and some would argue that they have stayed ruffled, though in changing settings, ever since. By the 18th century, even the traditional Christian belief that women were by nature more sinful than men was being revisited, with a growing argument that, since they were less involved in commerce, they were in fact more moral. This new view laid its own constraints on women, and could be accompanied by continued male superiority claims; but it was, in a quiet way, revolutionary.

The final big change in early modern Europe involved popular culture. Three major factors encouraged change. First, growing prosperity and commercialization could affect people's values. Family life, for example, won new praise when the quality of housing and furnishings improved (though remember, a large class of wage-earners did not enjoy this benefit). Physical comfort received new cultural esteem. For example, the use of umbrellas spread in England for the first time in the 18th century, and while some people complained that this undermined English hardiness, most agreed that staying dry was desirable – and this was a culture shift. Commercialization also increased competitiveness, which could heighten values associated with individualism (and also weaken community ties, including even friendships). Second, the printing press, plus the needs of a market economy, encouraged growing literacy, from the 16th century onward. By the 18th century, a higher percentage of West Europeans could read than anywhere else in the world except among whites in the British colonies of North America. Only a minority was involved even so, and it was disproportionately male; but lots of people now could read or had access to someone who did. This changed information sources and also encouraged new, possibly more structured ways to think about the world. Finally, the Scientific Revolution, quickly popularized, reduced the hold of religion and again encouraged a willingness to think in new ways.

Changes showed up at both elite and mass levels. Among elites, manners became more refined, from the Renaissance onward, in what one sociologist has called the "civilizing process." People became more aware that they should not burp and fart in public; toilet training became stricter and human urine, once prized, for example, as a good substance for tooth brushing, by the 18th century seemed disgusting; kissing (which as late as the 17th century involved frequent biting) became gentler and more private. Changes of this sort spread to the middle class and even below.

Naming practices shifted among ordinary people. In 1600 lots of children were not named until they were two (because so many died), and when they were named they often received names of relatives including brothers or sisters who had died. By 1750 almost all children were named quickly, sibling names were never reused, and there was a growing premium on finding novel names, rather than family or religious names. All this suggested a growing desire to recognize and encourage individuality. There was also, by the 18th century, an increasing belief and the validity and importance of love – for children, for courting couples. A woman who argued that she could never love a spouse her parents had picked out was simply out of luck in 1600, for marriage was not supposed to be based on love but on property arrangements, but by 1750 lots of parents would listen, and some law courts would overrule the parents if they did not. Love also interacted with growing consumerism. A woman who sought to rouse romantic interest would now be more likely to buy a stylish dress than to use a magic potion. Cultural change was wide-reaching, and it could be deeply personal.

Elite and popular interactions were involved in a fourth set of changes, besides growing individualism, new family values, and a civilizing process. In 1600, if a person lost a valued object, he or she would usually employ a local cunningman to use magic to try to find it. By 1750 cunningmen had largely disappeared, in favor of advertising in weekly newspapers, or going to newly established lost and found offices. Chance and accident, in other words, were being handled in new ways. More widely, the belief in witches, widespread in the early 17th century, began to disappear or at least go underground. Upper classes turned against witchcraft trials by 1700. Efforts to use magic either for harm or for good declined, at least in public; though considerable popular belief remained. Gradually also, people began to reduce a magic-based approach to health problems, in favor either of doctors or commercial remedies.

Even the definition of appropriate moods began to change. In the 16th and 17th centuries, many Europeans had praised a certain degree of melancholy, because it showed a detachment from things of this world and signaled religious humility. But by the 18th century many people were now urged to be cheerful. Smiling won new praise in part because better dental products for the first time promoted whiter teeth.

These were huge changes, involving very personal beliefs and practices. They added up to a growing valuation of individualism, a growing belief in the importance of emotion and the emotional qualities of family life, and a growing sense that nature was orderly or could be arranged by human foresight.

Moreover, the shifts of popular culture combined with changes in family life and gender relations, commercialization, and the growth of the state to make Western Europe, by the 18th century, an unusual kind of agricultural society, and also very different from the society it had been. This, in turn, raises twin questions: how did all this reposition the West in the world, and what did all this do to the definition of Western civilization?

Reprise: the West in the world

The various big changes in the West in the early modern period raise some vital problems of interpretation from the standpoint of the wider world. First, it becomes increasingly tempting to assume that Western civilization was becoming better than civilizations or societies elsewhere. Many of the changes, after all, created institutions and values that are still cherished today. To the extent Western Europe got them first, the resulting value judgment may seem obvious.

But there are some other vantage points. Some of the changes Europe was experiencing had already occurred in other societies; Europe was just catching up. Having more effective governments and trained bureaucracies was, for example, old hat in China. Indeed, a few Europeans understood that the Chinese led in such areas as merit examinations for bureaucrats (which would not become standard in the West until the 1870s). This does not mean that government growth and rationalization did not constitute a big change in terms of Western tradition; it does mean that the Western trends were not unique in the world. The same thing applies to better manners and more insistence on self-control. Many Asian societies had long practiced careful manners and, indeed, by their standards Westerners could still seem fairly boorish. Even the new love for children only gradually modified a continued emphasis on harsh discipline that many other groups – including American Indians, appalled at how often Europeans spanked their children – found odd. In paying more attention to young children, Europe was not necessarily breaking new ground in global terms. Once more: really important change in the West did not always mean novelty in the world.

Some changes also, though important, were not clearly desirable. The growing definition of a nation-state proved extremely important not just in Western but also in world history, because ultimately almost every area wanted this too. But the results were often harmful, in producing new intolerance of other nations and peoples, new motives for war, new competitiveness, and the destruction of older multinational units that previously had worked very well. The same applies to aspects, at least, of commercialization and individualism, which could easily be carried too far. Even the decline of magic was not entirely a good thing, for it robbed many people of very successful ways of interpreting and coping with the world; the replacements did not always work as well, at least in terms of providing comforting reassurance. (And all this in addition to Western activities in the wider world such as the Atlantic slave trade that would clearly condition how other people saw the West.)

Finally, other societies were changing rapidly too; the West was not entirely alone. The early modern centuries constituted a vital change point for Japan, for instance. Confucianism and secular values gained ground rapidly, and though feudalism remained the powers of the central state and its bureaucracy increased. Education spread, and literacy levels rose just under the gains occurring in Western Europe. It is crucial to remember that what was going on in the West was not the whole of world history, and that the West was not the only society displaying unusual flexibility.

The changes in the West did, however, inevitably spill over to other parts of the world, though the main impacts came after 1800. (Until that point, few other societies noticed what was happening in the West aside from some recognition of scientific advances and the new effectiveness of the state.) There were three complex interactions.

First, most obviously, the changes in the West gave Europeans new ways to judge other people, as they encountered them in exploration, trade, conquest, or missionary activity. Old criteria persisted: "others" could be judged harshly for not being Christian or for lagging in technology. But now their family habits, for example, or their superstitiousness might also be criticized. Europeans began to find the ways that women were treated in Asia reprehensible. Evidence of belief in magic in Africa was just one more sign of backwardness. Europeans divided on whether they thought these differences could and should be corrected, to bring "natives" up to "proper" civilized – i.e. Western – standards, or whether they were permanent signs of inferiority. But they certainly increased European self-satisfaction in the evaluation of the rest of the world – and some of this lingers even today.

Second, in part because European societies were becoming both confident and successful, the changes gave complex new targets for other societies to shoot at when and if they decided they wanted to copy the West. We have seen that the nation-state is a good example. While a few societies had long associated political activity with culture – China and Japan, most obviously – most had to make a big adjustment to think in nation-state terms. But, by the 19th and 20th centuries adjust they did as multinational empires such as the Ottoman and even the Russian empires were ultimately carved up. Western science was another important new target, noticed in Japan and the Ottoman empire even before 1800. But other targets might ultimately draw attention as well, such as the new Western valuation of love as a key component of male–female relationships.

But, third, some of the changes in the West would long seem undesirable in many other cultures, making a process of imitation, or even tolerance, more complicated. The emerging Western esteem for women's morality, in principle at least, was not self-evidently good to Japanese visitors to the West in the 19th century, who thought that Western women were given far too much credit. Individualism and commercialism might rouse hostile reactions as well.

The changes in the West, in sum, generated some love–hate reactions in other societies, sometimes even in the same individual, as they gradually became known thanks to increasingly intense interactions after 1800. Imitation and revulsion could coexist, depending on what aspect of the West was under discussion, or depending on the particular society or individual involved. And these complexities occurred even as many Westerners believed they had an increasing monopoly on all the criteria of modern civilization.

The trail of Western civilization

In terms of the West itself, what did these varied and profound changes do to a Western tradition? The basic answer is: it considerably transformed but did not obliterate it, which means that Western civ remained definable. It does not need to be fully reinvented, and it should not be seen as fully reinvented.

The key changes had three different relationships to the past. Some of them, quite simply, were new. They became important parts of the Western identity but they were truly products of change. The idea of a rationalized, bureaucratic state (granting that its emergence had just begun) was not a previous part of the Western tradition. It became Western, if not uniquely Western, now. The same holds for many, probably most, of the innovations in popular culture. The West now began to define itself, for example, in terms of cheerfulness and smiles, or a reverence for women's moral qualities, or the importance of consumer goods for ordinary people. These were unusual attributes of a civilization, and they were new to the West itself; they added significantly to the Western self-definition. The unusual aspects and consequences of the European-style family, which became such a distinctive feature of Western civilization, had no clear precedent in earlier Western patterns. It now became "Western" to think of families as primarily nuclear.

Another set of changes were also new but were prepared in part by earlier features of the West. The nation-state was novel; it became part of the Western political identity, though ultimately it was copied beyond the West. But the nation-state did emerge from the political divisions and internal warfare of earlier Western civilization. There had even been a few hints that Englishmen in the Middle Ages might recognize their Englishness – particularly when they were fighting the French, whom they already in the 15th century called "frogs" because of distinctive eating preferences. Luther, the first Reformation leader, appealed to Germanness in his fight against the Pope in Rome. So though the nation-state and nationalism were new highlights in Western civilization, they had some prior foundation. The same may apply to love. A cultural strand in the late Middle Ages had already idealized love, which became the subject for a good deal of poetry and song. The emphasis on love in the 18th century was both more intense and widespread; but it may have embraced some earlier Western ingredients. Consumerism was new to the Western identity. Several Asian societies had shown more signs of consumerism earlier, if only because they were more prosperous and had a more pleasure-seeking upper class. But Western eagerness for spices and other imports, even earlier, may have created a partial entryway for the later innovations.

A final set of shifts built quite explicitly on what the West already was. They involved change also, but here within a definable Western civilization. Here, particularly, is where the West did not entirely reinvent itself.

The Scientific Revolution was a revolution, in specific discoveries, in the ways science was defined and above all in the growing primacy of scientific thinking in Western intellectual life.

"Western science" became a new badge of identity, within the West and in the world at large, and this was unprecedented. But the new science heavily used elements inherited from Greek scientific thinking, as it had been revived, combined with Arab components, and rethought during the Middle Ages. It had a complex but partly Western foundation.

As with science earlier, there is real need for caution, lest the West seem to have a monopoly on rational thought. A key component of the new scientific revolution involved the discovery by the Polish monk, Copernicus, that the earth was not the center of the universe, but rather that the sun organized planetary motion in the solar system. He used careful mathematics to correct a long-standing Greek error (which reminds us that the Western scientific tradition has hardly been infallible). In fact, Chinese, Indian, and Mayan scientists had known about the sun's central role long before Copernicus. Arab mathematicians had also worked on this problem and had generated the two key discoveries Copernicus used, as early as the 13th century. Whether Copernicus copied (and concealed, perhaps because imitating Muslims was now shameful) or independently discovered, we do not know. But again, the complex relationship of the scientific revolution to Western and world history must be emphasized. This said, within the Western context Copernicus's findings were vital, as they were taken up by other scientists in the 17th century. They showed that tradition could be overturned by new thinking; they encouraged a new blend of rational theorizing and empirical obser-vation; and this, in turn, contributed to an unprecedented place for science in overall Western culture. Something distinctive was going on with Western science, but it was not all narrowly Western and, most important, it built on earlier Western thinking about the physical universe, about rationalism, even about some openness to (quietly) imitating science elsewhere.

The same kind of linkage applies to commercialization. Having commerce serve as a centerpiece for personal motives and social institutions was a new feature in Western civilization, again one for which the West became widely known around the globe. But commercialization was possible in part because of the merchant activity, and the distinctive place of merchants in urban life (and the willingness to copy commercial methods from the Arabs) that had emerged during the Middle Ages. There was a link to an earlier, if lower key, aspect of the civilization – without which, conceivably, the more modern commercialism could not have been built.

A Western tradition also persisted in politics, in terms of an ongoing impulse to provide some specific checks on the power of the state and the executive. Medieval methods, which relied on feudalism and the church, did not last in any literal sense. Indeed, absolutism threatened to overwhelm this Western tradition entirely. The 17th century French monarchy resolutely refused to call the central parliament, and it exerted new state powers over church and religion. But the tradition did not die. It was preserved in regional institutions and, of course, in the ongoing example of England and Holland. The results of the English Civil War, in the mid- to late 17th century, produced a more modern version of the older parliamentary institution. Political theory picked up the tradition as well. There was relatively little theoretical defense of strong state and monarch without qualification, though there was some. Dominant theory came to call for parliaments, constitutions, and definitions of some rights, including religions rights, that government should not touch – a significant change but also a recognizable link to the earlier Western idea of the state. With the French revolution of 1789, and ensuing European revolts (plus the American revolutionary example), theory was put into practice. Constitutions, declarations of rights, and parliaments became standard parts of the Western state, even as the state itself continued to expand. There was tension here, and recurrently some countries would drop the limits in favor of a barefaced assertion of state power. But on the whole, a Western commitment remained. Even nationalism proved double-edged; it provided new support for the state, but it also implied that the state required some connection to the people and a popular voice.

Overall, by 1800 "the West" meant a package of characteristics, some of them quite new and just being worked out, such as the idea of a loving family and a cherished wife and mother, some of them, such as merchant power and limited government, of earlier vintage though now greatly changed and updated. The early modern centuries were crucial to the Western identity, in demonstrating a capacity to innovate dramatically – sometimes for better, sometimes for worse – while maintaining some recognizable qualities. And it was also in the early modern centuries that the West, as a growing global power, developed a new capacity to separate the characteristics Western leaders themselves emphasized, from the cruder seizures of power and people Western adventurers perpetrated elsewhere in the world – a separation that would long complicate how the West saw itself in comparison to how it was seen by others.

Further reading

Norbert Elias, *The Civilizing Process* (New York: Pantheon Books, 1982); J. Hajnal, "European Marriage Patterns in Perspective" *Population in History* (1965); Peter Sahlins, *Boundaries: The Making of France and Spain in the Pyrenees* (Berkeley: University of California Press, 1989); Mary Hartman, *Re-imagining the Past: A Subversive View of Western History* (2003); Charles Tilly, *Big Structures, Large Processes, Huge Comparisons* (New York: Russell Sage Foundation, 1984); Colin Campbell, *The Romantic Ethic and the Spirit of Modern Consumerism* (Oxford, UK; New York, NY, USA: B. Blackwell, 1987); Keith Thomas, *Religion and the Decline of Magic: Studies in Popular Beliefs in Sixteenth and Seventeenth Century England* (Oxford: Oxford University Press, 1971).

Chapter 9

Where in the world was Western civilization?

Western civilization has always posed some geographical problems. We encountered these when we discussed the claims that classical Greece, largely eastward looking, presided over the origins of the West.

As Western civilization took further shape during the Middle Ages, further questions arose. What was the relationship of Spain, even as it was reconquered by Christians, to the West? Well into the 20th century, it has seemed just a bit different, when compared to "standard" Western norms. Even Italy, so important to the medieval West, lacked the full commitment to feudalism and other Western forms. Scandinavia, late in Christianization, was long another frontier, linked to the West but not part of its core. East central Europe poses another interpretive problem. Poland for example was Catholic, but somewhat distant from the Western core; was it fully Western? Ambiguous relationships for borderlands are common in defining civilization – it is a key issue for China, both past and present, particularly for its Western frontier with the many minority peoples and the significant presence of Islam. But the issue has some special twists for the West.

By the early modern period, the increasing formation of nation-states within the Western heartland raises yet another set of problems. Britain and France, for example, were obviously different, one Protestant, one Catholic, one committed to a rather small state (until the 20th century), the other firmly centralized. Were they equally Western? What about Germany, different yet again from France? Obviously, Western civilization has to acknowledge considerable internal regional diversity. This is hardly unprecedented; the same applies to Indian civilization through history. But it is a bit messy.

This chapter deals with a somewhat different kind of geographical issue, which took shape because of the West's growing success. Three different kinds of societies began to develop a special kind of relationship with Western Europe during the early modern period, and this has extended into modern times. In each case, the question has been raised by historians and people in each of the societies: did this society also become Western? And in each case, the question is both interesting and legitimate – though the answers may vary.

(Note that the issue of new territories in an expanding civilization is hardly confined to the West. Most obviously: is there an Islamic civilization, or a Middle Eastern civilization plus Islam in other societies such as Africa or southeast Asia?)

Here we take up three different possibilities for inclusion, in terms of expansion well after the origins of Western civilization itself: Russia and eastern Europe, Latin America, and the so-called settler societies including the United States. Some additional societies, mainly more recently, have also copied the West extensively, but they are less likely candidates, because they preserve so much separate tradition. And in any event they can best be discussed in a later chapter, on globalization, because whatever issues they raise are mostly fairly recent.

One final preliminary: in talking about whether another society is Western or not, it is important to remember that the ability to be Western is not necessarily the highest praise one can offer in world history, nor is a difference from the West, despite exposure, the sign of some weakness or fault. Societies, or individuals within them, can quite rationally decide they do not want to be Western, even when they have a chance. As the West gained world prominence it held itself as a standard of maximum civilization, and many other people agreed. So it is undeniably difficult to talk about possible non-Westernness without seeming to criticize. We must nevertheless make the attempt.

Russia and eastern Europe

Russia is a really interesting case because, of course, much of it is in Europe. Those Western civ textbooks that are essentially European history usually include Russia without explicit assessment, though they usually devote less space to it, which suggests some degree of uncertainty. On another level: the great French leader Charles de Gaulle, in the 1950s and 1960s, when he was trying to free France from undue American control, used to talk about the oneness of Europe – Europe to the Urals. The implication was that Europe should figure out its commonalities, as opposed to Cold War distinctions between the two sides of the Iron Curtain: Western and communist. So the issue is not just a challenge to European historians, but to policymakers as well. For their part world historians are often uncertain what to do with Russia, in part because of its European overlap.

The dilemma is not terribly acute for the Middle Ages. Eastern Europe was Christian, like the West, but its Orthodox version of Christianity was different, whether the topic was marriage of priests or the relationship of church and state. More important, European trade at this point went largely south–north, rather than east–west. The trade route through western Russia and Ukraine headed to Constantinople; exchanges with the West were limited, in part, of course, because the West had so little to offer. Eastern

Europe did not develop feudalism; it did not emphasize sea trade; while it, too, drew on a Greco–Roman classical past it emphasized the Greek part, and its artistic styles were distinctive as a result. It was simply operating in a different, east European, civilization zone culturally and commercially dominated by the Byzantine empire. When Russia was largely overrun by the Mongols in the 14th century, this further confirmed the separation between the two main European regions.

But when Russia revived, after 1450, regaining independence and beginning its long process of expansion, the situation was different. Among other things the Byzantine Empire was gone, which removed a key model. By the late 15th century Russian tsars were in active contact with the West, inviting Renaissance Italian architects in to help design the Kremlin, where they blended Italian and traditional Russian styles to create monuments of exceptional beauty. While Russia maintained strong Asian influences and interests, as its expansion pushed farther into central and eastern Asia, the sense of the West's relevance undoubtedly increased. Trade with the West began to expand as well, though on a decidedly unequal basis. Not only did Russia export crude products, such as furs, in return for Western goods, but also the trade was handled by Western merchants who insisted, colonial-style, on regulating themselves by their laws rather than Russia's.

The real questions about Westernization begin, of course, with Peter the Great in the late 17th century. Peter greatly expanded the sense of West as model. At this time also Russia became an active player in European diplomacy and military affairs for the first time. There was little direct power-bloc connection with countries such as France as yet – this would not come until the revolutionary wars around 1800. But Russia's competition with central European powers such as Sweden and Prussia, as well as with Poland, bring the giant nation clearly into the European history survey textbooks for the first time at this point.

Moreover, Peter's reforms pushed Russia into a clearly Western orbit, quite apart from wars and diplomacy, in one and perhaps two ways. Russia began to participate in Western high culture. Initially this was simply as an importer, of Western forms such as the ballet, painting and literacy styles, Christmas trees, and clothing fashions. Upper-class Russians completed their education by prolonged travel in the West, to see what real civilization was like; sometimes, they spoke only French, ignorant of Russian. By the early 19th century the overlap went further. Russian intellectuals began to contribute actively, often brilliantly, to Western intellectual life. Poets such as Pushkin, political writers such as Herzen, composers such as Tchaikovsky were part of a common intellectual scene, widely enjoyed by Westerners if only in translation. Of course there was a bit of Russian flavor involved, but the Western experience always juggled common elements with national distinctions. Russia also participated in Western science, again importing discoveries and institutional forms, such as scientific academies, in the 18th century, and then contributing actively to a common scientific body of work by the 19th century. By the end of the 19th century scientists such as Pavlov were making fundamental discoveries as part of a European scientific community. A second connection was more limited. Peter and his successors imported Western political forms copied from absolutism, which increased bureaucratic efficiency and training. They shared an appetite for military rivalry. While in fact, the Russian state was weaker than its absolutist counterparts in Prussia or France, because of the vast territory involved and the huge powers landlords wielded directly over serfs, it is possible to sketch some common aspects of Russian and European political history from the late 17th century until about 1848. By the latter point, the impact of Western revolutions even on conservative states such as Prussia, in forcing certain key reforms, combined with Russia's resolute resistance to revolutionary contagion, reduced the political overlap. Except for the few months of liberal control in the Revolution of 1917 (noteworthy for its brevity), Russian and Western political patterns would continue to remain separate until – with lots of question marks – the 1990s.

But there was more to Russian Westernness than growing trade and diplomatic ties, the real participation in Western culture as creator as well as consumer, and a period of political contact. By the late 18th century significant numbers of upper-class and intellectual Russians saw the West as Russia's model, urging that Russia become more thoroughly Western in social and political structure. They judged their society backward because Westerners saw it so, and they wanted to break through to full participation in Western forms.

Overall, however, Russia was European (though also partly Asian) but not Western. The political gaps, save during the absolutist period, are one sign. Limitations on Peter's reforms, however, loom even larger. Peter did not want to create a large merchant class, lest he antagonize his aristocracy. He did spur certain kinds of manufacturing, particularly where relevant to military strength. And Russian explorers, seeking new trade patterns in the Pacific, for example, where their expeditions took them to North America and even to Hawaii, have something in common with Western adventurers in the same period. But Russia did not seek to become a significant player in world, as opposed to regional, trade, and it did not shake its dependence on Western merchants. Its trade relationship with the West involved low-cost exports, in grain, for example, based on cheap labor, in return for more complex luxury products and equipment. A hope for full participation in the world economy in parity with the West flickered perhaps around 1900, in the minds of eager industrial leaders like Count Witte, and again in the 1990s, but it has yet to become reality. Russian social structure, similarly, long remained distinctive. Far less urban than the West, Russia also long maintained a rigid serfdom and, even after its abolition in 1861, experienced a significant set of peasant problems that would mark it off from the West. Industrialization, mainly in the 20th century, created some social convergence. Even under communism, a clear middle as well as working class emerged; urban families faced issues, such as reducing the birth rate, that were also similar to those in the West. But Russian society, no more than the state or the economy, was not Western. And Russian popular culture, virtually untouched by Peter the Great, also long remained distinctive. Russian peasants did not undergo the kind of popular cultural transformation, including a reduction of religious influence, that their Western counterparts experienced by the 18th century. Again, with growing literacy by the very late 19th century, a greater overlap began to emerge. This increased still further, late in the 20th century, when Western consumer influences gained greater penetration. But significant gaps persisted.

Finally, in reaction to Peter the Great and recurrently since, Russia also developed a pronounced hostility to the West, that often balanced, or even overbalanced, the sense of West as model. By the 1730s, Orthodox priests were urging Russian leaders to pull back, for Westernization would loosen Russia from its true values. Soon, conservative landlords were also insisting that Western social forms, particularly when heightened by revolutionary principles, were dangerously unRussian: Russian serfs needed their masters for they could not survive on their own. By the mid-19th century, Russian conservative nationalists went even further, in arguing not only against Westernization, but also in favor of the superiority of Russian values. A number of statements attacked the West for its political instability and foolish reliance on parliamentary and democratic institutions, for its commercial exploitation, social injustice, and materialism, and for excessive individualism. Russia's true spirituality and sense of community, beginning with the peasant village, as well as its absolutist state were held up as preferable models, at least for Russia, for Slavic peoples more generally, and perhaps, should they ever awaken from their mad dash to modernity, for the West itself. In the 20th century, particularly under Stalin, communist rhetoric created another set of attacks on the West, seizing again on individualism, class exploitation, and materialism while adding some new points such as the addiction to sterile modernism in the arts.

Critics of Western values arose in the West as well. Communism united many Russians with passionate Western opponents of capitalism. German conservatives, hostile to democracy and to "French" innovations such as the department stores, shared worries with their Russian counterparts in the late 19th century. But the deep ambivalence about the West, the attraction and repulsion, that became such a basic part of Russian history from about 1700 onward, never fully described more purely Western regions. And this is the final reason to contend that, though certainly European and a vital part of European history, Russia and the West have not yet merged. The question of Russia as Western raises some valid issues, worth exploring, but ultimately it is a non-starter in modern history to date. Russia is best treated, analytically, as a separate civilization tradition.

Three final points. First, Russia as not Western is not a value judgment. The Russians who insisted, and insist still, that some of their values are superior are worth listening to. It is obviously true that Russia's lack of full Westernness has, again since Peter the Great, been associated with backwardness, in many Western eyes and in Russian eyes as well. But excluding Russia from full Western history need not be taken as a criticism.

Nor, second, should the judgment be taken as a prediction that Russia will never become Western. Societies can change, and Russia is changing rapidly today – though the ambivalence about the West remains, from political leaders anxious about their own authority to ordinary people who regret the loss of welfare protections and the greater sense of equality of the communist era. Other societies that once were not fully Western have become so – Greece and Spain are clear examples in the later 20th century. Russia's long history of Western overlap may lead to greater identity, and certainly many contemporary Russians wish this to occur.

Finally, there is the truly knotty question of Eastern Europe outside Russia. Currently, large number of eastern Europeans – or, as they much prefer to be called, central Europeans – are eager to associate their histories with those of the West, just as they seek membership in Western institutions such as the European Union and NATO. Often, part of their argument insists on their differences from Russia, whose period of post-World-War-II control is deeply resented still. Part of east–central Europe, notably Poland, Hungary, the Czech and Slovak Republics, Slovenia, Croatia, and the Baltic states, are also Western in religious tradition, Catholic or (in Hungary and the Baltic) partly Protestant. Many of them, such as Poland with the great scientist, Copernicus, participated in the Scientific Revolution (unlike Russia) as well as the Enlightenment. Some clearly shared in Western political values besides nationalism – the Czech republic, as the only east–central European country to develop a viable democratic and parliamentary state between the World Wars, has the most impressive claims here.

On the other hand, during long stretches of modern history east–central Europe differed greatly from the West in dominant social and economic structures – where the resemblance to Russia was considerable. Large peasantries, long ensnared in serfdom (Romania, for example, extricated itself from serfdom even later than Russia), combined with a pattern of exporting food and raw materials and importing more expensive Western items. Even with the advent of free market economies since 1991, the huge economic gap with the West persists. This, along with a distinctive political history partly because of long periods of external control by Russia, Austria, or the Ottoman Empire, does raise some questions.

There is no doubt that most east–central Europeans now want to be Western. Their opportunities to become so are probably greater than those of Russia if only because of greater historical overlap. But even today, and certainly in modern history more generally, the question of where to locate the West's eastern boundary – and the question of what criteria to use in trying to define it – is not an easy one. We have to allow for a certain degree of sloppiness, and for the possibility of both fluctuation and debate.

Latin America

A few years ago Latin American historians in the United States conducted an active internet discussion over whether the society they study should be thought of as a separate civilization or as part of the West. The discussion has some components similar to those involved in the Russian case, but inevitably there are distinctive features as well.

Unlike Russia, for example, Latin America was converted to a clearly Western version of Christianity. Even by the late 20th century, with Protestant fundamentalism spreading rapidly, Western religious forms remained deeply influential. Of course, American Indian and African religious beliefs and practices blended with the Catholic, creating some important syncretic religions that were not found in Europe or even the United States. Of course, religious intensity (whether Catholic, Protestant, or syncretic) turned out, by the late 19th and 20th centuries, to be greater in Latin America than in Europe. Secular interests and Enlightenment values, though also easily accepted by some Latin Americans, advanced less far. But the degree of religious sharing, in this vital aspect of cultural and institutional life, was and is considerable.

There was also a significant overlap in terms of political traditions, and particularly liberalism. Again unlike Russia, Latin America participated actively in the wave of Atlantic revolutions after 1800. Enlightenment and French and American revolutionary political ideas spread to many leadership groups. Liberal issues, such as education, control of the church, and provision of constitutional and parliamentary regimes, form a key part of Latin America's political history in the 19th century, as they do in Europe and the United States. Latin America did have greater problems of political stability than Western Europe did, with more periods of strongman rule – though Spain and Portugal had some similar experiences. Faced with distinctive issues like what to do with Indians, Latin American liberals could be quite illiberal, insisting on forced change or strict controls. Partly because of this, Latin American liberals accepted democratic principles more slowly than their European counterparts – though European liberalism, too, long hesitated over widening the vote. Finally, the battles with conservatives, who represented church, landlord and military powers combined, were more persistent and ran deeper than was the case in most of 19th century Western Europe (Spain, again, partly excepted). None of this erases the importance of a liberal tradition in Latin America that has surfaced again in the 20th century.

Latin America's final big claim to Westernness resembles that of Russia: the substantial overlap in high culture, bolstered by the fact many Latin

Americans, particularly though not exclusively in the upper classes, were fully European in origin and traveled in Western Europe extensively. Art and architecture were heavily Western. The Latin American literary tradition, as it emerged in the 19th century, relied greatly on Western (particularly French) forms, and it contributed to Western culture in turn. Again as with Russia there were some distinctive themes and flavors, but the amount of mutual exchange remained considerable. Music and dance were somewhat different. Latin American cities created Western orchestras eager to participate in the classical music canon, but specifically Latin American contributions to more popular music and dance styles reflected different origins. Still, many middle- and upper-class Latin Americans have long thought of themselves as Western and have sought to Westernize their countries. In the later 19th century, particularly in places like Argentina or Chile where the European presence was particularly strong, cityscapes were Westernized, along with Western-style campaigns against disease, prostitution and a host of other conditions. Cities such as Buenos Aires were hard to distinguish from their Western counter- parts. As in Russia again, a sense of backwardness existed, defined in terms of the gaps between Latin America and the European West, but the standards or goals seemed identical.

So why hesitate? Again as with Russia, the chief reasons involve social and economic forms. Indeed, Latin America was far slower to industrialize than Russia was, which suggests even greater distinctions in this area. Latin America was quickly established as a colonial, dependent economy, with a large, exploited rural population and relatively small cities and merchant classes. Europeans and, soon, US Americans called most of the key economic shots. Dependence on raw materials and on cash crops such as coffee persisted well into the 20th century. Leaders, many of them liberal, struggled mightily to escape this vice, but on the whole dependence got worse rather than better at least until the later 1930s. And huge vestiges remain today, even in countries like Mexico and Brazil that have now built significant industrial sectors. And, of course, a distinctive set of economic and social patterns inevitably spills over into politics and culture. One of the reasons for greater Latin American religiosity involves the depth of extensive poverty. One of the reasons that liberal states have been, on the whole, somewhat harder to construct involves the bitterness of divisions between landlords and peasants. It is hard to write Latin America into Western history using the same chapter headings.

More than Russia, however, this is a mixed case. Ironically, because it is not in Europe, Latin America is less often included in comments on the evolution of Western civilization than eastern Europe is. Without wiping away the distinctions – and the desirability of considering Latin America, on balance, as a separate civilization – we need to make this aspect of the Western civ canon a bit more flexible. There are serious and interesting issues involved. And there is the possibility of further assimilation in future. As Latin

America participates in global economic institutions – at a disadvantage, but with some prospects for improvement; and as it leads in late 20th century conversions to liberal, democratic political forms – the questions about Westernness need to remain open-ended.

Settler societies and the United States

Canada, Australia, New Zealand, and the United States all developed on the basis of widespread reduction of indigenous populations, because of conquest and disease, combined with large-scale immigration of European populations. As settler societies they differ from Latin America, where the Indian component on the whole remained stronger because the prior populations were larger. Their primary political and economic contact with Britain rather than Spain added another ingredient, helping to explain, for example, why they more easily developed parliamentary political forms given Britain's firmer tradition in this regard, and possibly why they more readily established a large merchant class.

The question is: were they Western? For if they were, the West begins to expand massively by the 17th and 18th centuries. The Western civ tradition itself assumed a key link, at least between the United States and Western civilization, but ironically rarely explored it: it was not clear whether Western values and institutions sat at the foundation of these new societies, which then went their own way while possibly improving on the original, or whether there was an ongoing participation in a single civilization.

We can begin by building on the discussion of Latin America. The settler societies, including the United States, shared religion with the West, though in this case majority Protestantism rather than Catholicism. They shared political traditions. The American revolution extended colonial experience with legislatures and Enlightenment political theory. To prevent similar separations in Canada and, later, Australia, Britain encouraged an independent national parliamentary tradition which led, later in the 19th century, to effective political independence but with a set of institutions very similar to those of the motherland. Finally, elite culture participated heavily in larger Western forms. The settler societies were initially too primitive to do much in the way of independent art or literature. Early on, however, colonial Americans were exceptionally active participants in the Enlightenment and in scientific inquiry. As prosperity and experience accumulated, furthermore, adoption of basically European forms in painting, architecture, classical music, and literature proceeded rapidly. As with Latin America, there were some distinctive themes, reflecting for example frontier experience. The United States also, ultimately, contributed innovations based on the African-American heritage, particularly in music. But there is no question that, overall, intellectual and artistic life in the settler societies formed part of a common Western experience, with lots of mutual exchange and travel, particularly of Americans to Western artistic meccas such as Paris.

In contrast to Latin America, the settler societies did not generate dependent economies. They continued to emphasize agriculture and mining more than Western Europe did. But they handled much of the trade on their own, with their own growing business classes. Using vast tracts of lands and extensive mechanization, they did not rely on a low-wage labor force to the extent pervasive in Latin America. Furthermore, particularly in the United States, they quickly began to industrialize, which further reduced economic inferiority. United States industrialization, copied from Britain because of unusually fruitful contacts, proceeded with much the same timing, and along many of the same lines, as that of France or Germany. There were a few distinctions, including extensive reliance on European capital markets for investment funds. The American South, with slavery, was a much more dependent economy than was characteristic of the rest of the United States or of the other settler societies that avoided extensive slavery. On balance, however, economic patterns tended to link with, rather than dissociate from, the Western heartland.

Still, however, there are issues. Some of them result from the practical effects of the tradition of teaching US history separately from Western or world history. It is easy to assume separate patterns because of separate treatment. More broadly, however, an interpretive tradition, called American exceptionalism, explicitly tries to distinguish American from Western history while admitting important initial inspiration and connections. According to the exceptionalist argument, there were various reasons that the United States began to depart from European models (usually in good ways, though the argument does not depend on this).

As an example: there is no question that the United States did not generate a serious socialist movement, despite some modest beginnings in the late 19th century. This differentiated the United States from literally the entire Western world, including Australia and New Zealand, and from many other societies as well. Why? Answers include the ethnic variations within the American working class, which reduced mutual understanding, strong pressure from the middle class and the state that viewed socialism as scary and foreign and used strong police and propaganda pressure to inhibit it, and a belief that American society was particularly mobile, and that, given individual opportunity, socialism was not needed. Note that actual mobility was not much different from that in Western Europe, but Europeans tended to downplay mobility chances, claiming social blockage, whereas Americans, to this day, tend to exaggerate the amount of mobility available and blame individuals, rather than social conditions, for failures to advance. Correspondingly, by the later 20th century almost all Americans (85%) claimed they were middle class, while many Europeans continued to note with pride that they were working class – even though jobs structures and standards of living differed very little between the two regions. Here, obviously, a small comparison yields a rich differentiation between the United States and the rest of the West. And there are further consequences: without socialism, the United States also failed in the 20th century to develop a full welfare state, again in contrast to the rest of the West. Even Canada generated national health insurance, which the United States continues to shun.

There are many other arrows in the exceptionalist quiver, though few of them have been tested as carefully through comparison as in the case of socialism. Is the United States its own civilization, as the existence of "American civilization" programs in many universities suggests? What are the best arguments? While a full analysis would require a book in itself, a few guidelines can be suggested.

Several of the main differences between the United States and standard Western civilization involve the impacts of the frontier and of racial/ethnic diversity, including in this latter the existence of slavery and its legacy of racial bitterness even after abolition. Some of these factors also existed in Latin America. Thus from the 18th century until at least very recently, the United States has been far more violent, per capita, than Western Europe – more like Latin America in this regard. Both frontier conditions and racial hostilities fed this characteristic, and the ongoing difference in regulation of guns (with Europe far more comfortable with gun control) both reflects and confirms it. From the outset, and still today, Americans have also been more geographically mobile than West Europeans. On the other hand, partly because of weaker community ties and more ethnic diversity, Americans by the 19th century were more religious than West Europeans. A clearer separation between churches and politics contributed to this as well, but the importance of religion for identity and community was particularly striking. By the late 20th century Americans were about five times more likely than Europeans to be active church, temple, or mosque goers and to profess active religious belief.

Greater ethnic diversity and undeniable racial issues in the United States must not be seen solely in terms of strife. Like Latin America, the United States also benefited from the cultural contributions of peoples from Africa and from native Americans, with significant innovations in a variety of artistic fields – some of which, such as jazz, were enthusiastically imported into Western Europe later on.

Other key differences relate to the absence of a real aristocracy and peasantry in the United States. The United States has been middle-class dominated virtually since its inception, apart from the hold of southern gentry and of Dutch landowners in upstate New York. While the United States often tolerates more extreme inequalities in wealth than Western Europe maintained, it is less open to overt social snobbery, more insistent on at least superficial egalitarianism in manners (though racial tensions can complicate this). The importance of measuring achievement by wealth and of approving of wealth-getting tactics has also been greater in the United States, because of the absence of a real alternative through a separate aristocratic standard.

Some differences, also real, should not be pressed too far. It is interesting that Americans developed baseball and football rather than soccer as national sports passions, but the timing of the sports enthusiasms, including the rise of professional sports, and the basic social meanings were very similar on both sides of the Atlantic. Different surface manifestations, in other words, but same dynamic. We have seen that, despite significantly different ideas about social mobility, actual experiences were very similar. Careful comparative studies have shown that, in the 19th century, rates of upward mobility, to higher social and economic levels than the family of origin, were virtually identical, though there was less downward mobility in the United States; in the 20th century, even this distinction disappeared.

Political democracy was another overlap area. Extensions of the vote to adult males (other than slaves) occurred first in France in 1792–93, though the revolutionary experiment was shortlived. Many northern American states moved to democracy by the 1820s, about two decades before the next European step (in France, in 1848). Germany and England were essentially on board by the 1860s, though with different specific political systems. These distinctions in timing are not insignificant, but they should not obscure the fact of a general movement within a half-century span, based on new demands from ordinary people in industrializing societies and on the continuing inspiration of Enlightenment ideas on both sides of the Atlantic. Similar patterns describe massive educational change. Northern states in the United States moved more quickly to obligatory mass education than did most of Europe, which on the other hand maintained clearer elite training tracks. But by the 1870s mass education was a fact of life on both sides of the Atlantic, along with virtually universal literacy, while the United States was directly copying the German model of the research university.

And a host of major trends, some of them involving quite personal behaviors, occurred essentially in parallel, suggesting significant cohesion within an expanded Western civilization. The industrial revolution, though launched in Britain, turned out to be a transatlantic process very quickly. Again, different regions had different specific emphases: the British government, for example, did less to promote industrialization directly than the United States government did (with its huge grants of land to railroads), which, in turn, did less than the German. But the timing and results were very similar. The same applies to the new movement to limit per capita birth rates – the demographic transition that ran through Western civilization during the 19th century. American birth rates were a bit higher than European when this development began, thanks to more available land, but reductions began by the 1790s, just a bit after France but before Britain, and the outcomes by 1900, in unprecedentedly low birth rates per family combined with rapidly falling infant death rates, was essentially the same throughout this expanded Western world. And this resulted not from some deliberate, imitative government policy, but from spontaneous commonalities in the decisions made by hosts of ordinary families. Women's developments also moved in parallel. Western industrialization reduced the role of women in the formal labor force – Britain and the United States moved faster here than France did. But there was growing pressure for new legal rights. Feminist movements cropped up on both sides of the Atlantic, and again developments in the United States, Britain and Scandinavia (areas of Protestant dominance) resembled each other more than other parts of the Western world, such as France, where Catholic traditions held. By the 1920s women had gained voting rights in the United States, Scandinavia, Britain, Germany (and also Australia and New Zealand). Parallels would continue in the 20th century, with virtually identical patterns of reentry of married women into the labor force in the 1950s and 1960s, very similar incidence of a youth "sexual revolution" in the 1960s, and so on.

The obvious point is, thanks to shared though not identical origins, shared processes such as industrialization, and continued, close contact in fields like women's rights or medicine, it is accurate to speak of a common, expanded Western civilization in many respects. Australia, New Zealand and Canada, without the slavery experience that so marked United States history, but also without quite such rapid industrialization, participated in this pattern as well. Important differences existed, though they were not always greater than those among European nations themselves. On balance, however, there are fewer issues in this particular Western civ category than we encountered in dealing with Russia or Latin America.

Conclusion

The American exceptionalist debate is an important component of any analysis of the modern history of Western civilization. It forces Americans, some of whom are simultaneously proud of their society's presumed Western origins and eager to dissociate themselves from aspects of Western Europe they do not like, really to think about what their civilization identity is and how it has evolved historically. A case can be made for both sides in the debate, when reasonably precise comparison is applied. And we will see that the discussion must be resumed when we turn more fully to the 20th century. But a Western civ argument is defendable.

During the 18th and 19th centuries, Western civilization expanded geographically, in whole or in part. Some regions involved can best be regarded as separate civilizations with unusual overlaps and affinities with the West; others may be considered part of Western civilization itself, perhaps with an asterisk to denote special tensions and features. By the late 19th century, when the United States began to share West European interests in imperialist expansion as well as global economic activities, people in other societies might easily see the two power centers as one.

Further reading

Thomas E. Skidmore and Peter H. Smith, *Modern Latin America* (New York: Oxford University Press, 1997); John H. M. Laslett and Seymour Martin Lipset, ed. *Failure of a Dream? Essays in the History of American Socialism* (Berkeley: University of California Press, 1974); Seymour Martin Lipset, *American Exceptionalism: A Double-Edged Sword* (New York: W. W. Norton, 1996); Nicholas V. Riasanouvsky, *A History of Russia* (New York: Oxford University Press, 1993); John H. M. Laslett, *Colliers Across the Sea: A Comparative Study of Class Formation in Scotland and the American Midwest* (Urbana: University of Illinois Press, 2000); Jürgen Kocka, *White Collar Workers in America, 1890–1940: A Social–Political History in International Perspective* (London; Beverly Hills: Sage Publications, 1980); Peter Kolchin, *Unfree Labor: American Slavery and Russian Serfdom* (Cambridge, Mass.: Belknap Press of Harvard University Press, 1987).

Part IV

The West in the contemporary world

The idea of civilization may get lost in turning to the great events of contemporary history. Many world history courses carefully trace Chinese or African civilization into the 19th and 20th centuries, and then turn to different kinds of categories like colonialism, or economic underdevelopment, or world war. There is legitimate question as to whether civilization units work as well, analytically, in the contemporary period, as they did earlier on – particularly because of the undeniable intensification of cross-civilization contacts and imitations. These issues are legitimately applied to Western civilization. We have seen that one of the reasons that Western civ courses were created, in precisely this same contemporary era, was because of a fear that the Western position and identity were in fact eroding.

Chapters in this final section deal with the West in industrialization – a massive transformation that the West originated, but that in turn changed the West and its world position considerably. We then turn to the 20th century as a unit in Western history, when Western values and institutions for a time seemed threatened with extinction. We end with the issue of globalization, another process, like industrialization, that the West in many respects leads but that may challenge its identity. If, as some began to argue by the 1980s, the later 20th century sees a Westernization of the world, is there still a definable Western civilization left?

Chapter 10

Western civilization and the industrial revolution

It is no secret that the industrial revolution began in the West, first in Britain and then spreading quickly to Belgium, France, the United States, and Germany. By the 1850s, amid great regional variations, this was clearly becoming a Western-wide phenomenon. The result greatly enhanced the West's power in the wider world. Societies that were not Western, by origin or adoption, proved unable to join the industrial parade until the 1890s at the earliest, and some have not fully signed up even today.

Yet the industrial revolution is not usually explored in Western civ terms. Textbooks insert it into European or American history, along with political revolutions and other developments, but they rarely explicitly discuss the huge change in terms of civilizational causes and even more rarely discuss the civilizational results. A few analyses have attempted to explore why other societies did not industrialize first – China is the most interesting case, because of its good resources, technology tradition, and advanced commerce – but it is obviously hard to assign causes to something that did not happen. Still the effort properly reminds us that we need a comparative approach to explaining the industrial revolution, that will address the first key question: Why the West? We can then turn to what is perhaps even more interesting and significant, about the impact on Western traditions and identities. For it was the industrial revolution, more than any other single development, that launched the West in the contemporary world.

Definitions

The industrial revolution centered on a massive increase in production, and the related acceleration of transportation, communication, and sales capacities. Its heart lay in new technology, particularly technology based on coal (steam) or waterpower replacing human or animal power. Thus in the 18th century, the flying shuttle was a device that automatically carried the thread on a weaving loom across the fibers, so that a weaver could run the loom without an assistant. Result: at least 50% more cloth production per worker. Ultimately, this device could be linked to steam power, which increased the speed and the number of looms per machine, which upped the ante still further. By the late 19th century a single worker could tend 8 to 16 mechanical looms.

Massive increases in production also resulted from new work arrangements. Factories allowed more specialization of labor, which speeded output, and more direct supervision of work. These principles spread to other areas, such as department stores for sales, where new mechanization was not directly involved. Again, the result was faster work and quantitatively greater results.

With industrialization, manufacturing began to gain on agriculture as a source of jobs and wealth, and ultimately surpassed it. Older types of manufacturing, through skilled craft work or home-based production, gradually declined. Wealth and products per person increased, though because of great inequality poverty might grow for some groups as well. Rapid urbanization also accompanied industrialization, and Western society became 50% or more urban for the first time in human history, from about 1850 onward – first in Britain, then elsewhere.

A barebones definition of the industrial revolution does not do justice to the process. This was a huge change in the way people lived. Though it took 60–100 years to develop fully in any given region, the end result was truly revolutionary, one of the great alterations in human experience, comparable to the conversion from hunting and gathering to agriculture several millennia before. We will get at other aspects of the process in discussing its Western components.

Causes

Historians have worked on some of the reasons that Great Britain led the pack in the industrial revolution. Great Britain had an unusually commercially-minded aristocracy, which directly participated in some industrial operations and tolerated middle-class endeavors as well. The state was not heavily involved in economic regulation, compared to France, and artisans had considerable latitude to introduce technological innovations. Britain was running out of timber by the 18th century, which particularly pushed for greater use of coal and further development of coal mines. Britain also had excellent resources in iron and coal, and rivers helped these two essential industrial ingredients to be combined relatively easily; only Germany, Belgium, and parts of the United States, in the Western world, rivaled this resource position. Unusually wide colonial holdings brought capital, raw materials (such as Indian cotton), and potential markets. Britain also avoided the worst disruptions of the French revolutionary period, which set back the economies of the western part of the continent. Indeed, the revolutionary wars encouraged British industrial growth, while demonstrating to the rest of Europe the military and economic resources that industrialization could provide.

Because of the dominance of national histories in the European history tradition, many commentators have approached industrialization on a case-by-case basis, as if each experience was unique. France, with a more heavy-handed government, slower population growth, and less adequate holdings in coal and iron, industrialized not only later but a bit more slowly than Britain and Belgium. Its manufacturing long retained a more artisanal quality, though craft work itself was accelerated and standardized on industrial principles. Germany placed unusual emphasis on government intervention, on the promotion of huge corporate combinations or cartels, and on heavy industry. While Germany started a bit late, its focus (including strong concentration on providing technical education) allowed it to catch and begin to pass Britain by the late 19th century, as the British capacity for initial innovation was not matched by a full ability to keep up with more advanced industrial forms. Some regions on the fringes of Western Europe industrialized more slowly, or in regional pockets that did not quickly engage the whole country. This was the pattern in Spain, where industrialization occurred fairly early around Barcelona (in textiles) and around Bilbao in heavy industry, while the nation as a whole lagged. Sweden industrialized fairly early, but developments in Finland were much slower. Holland, despite or perhaps because of its great commercial success, was late in getting on the industrial train, and remained an oddly conservative society through most of the 19th century. And, of course, causes for all the national and regional patterns can be sought, following on the special assessment of the British leadership role.

But there is no reason to divide too finely. For what it really impressive about industrialization was its rapid spread through most of the Western world – and the lag of other regions outside the West, even when a few pilot factories were fairly quickly introduced. Russia, for example, had some railway lines and model factories by 1850, brought in by West Europeans or Americans; but in no sense did it begin a serious overall industrialization process until the 1890s. The same applies to Latin America. In contrast, it took only 40–50 years for the bulk of Western society to follow Britain's lead, despite British efforts to ban export of new machinery and machine designs and to keep skilled workers at home.

So, granting a need to explain Britain with some special factors, and to note other regional variants, the key questions are why the West, and what industrialization had to do with the nature of Western civilization.

Western society enjoyed a mixture of preconditions and causes for industrialization, and the distinction is useful. It is very difficult to industrialize without ready access to basic raw materials, and in the initial industrial revolution this meant coal and iron above all. (Later, when established industrial models could be imitated, Japan industrialized even though its domestic resource base was exceptionally poor.) Many parts of Europe, particularly along the coal seam that runs from Britain to the Ruhr in

Germany, had excellent holdings of coal and iron, often in proximity. This was vital to industrialization, but obviously it did not cause it – for the resources had been in the ground for ages without this use resulting. Resources do, however, help explain why Europe came first compared, say, to Japan, or the Middle East, or several other places.

There are three kinds of active explanations for the Western lead in industrialization. They can be combined in various ways, and almost certainly none is entirely adequate by itself. Only one of the explanations, however, seriously emphasizes distinctively Western qualities as opposed to more impersonal factors.

Approach 1

This was developed most extensively in recent years and stresses global causes, arguing that the West industrialized not because of special values or institutions but because of the unusual power position that it had achieved in world trade. Europe had already pushed its way toward commercial dominance, though it was still motivated by incomplete success in Asia. It learned from its trade position how much more money could be made from exporting manufactured goods, and importing cheaper raw materials. Industrialization merely extended this process, without any special Western qualities involved save perhaps greed and prior commercial success. Europe had also won massive profits from prior world trade, including the Atlantic slave trade, and these were begging for new investment opportunities. No other society had the capital required for initial risky investments in machinery. Again, no special Western values are involved here beyond an understanding of how to exploit other areas and a belief that this was fully justified, based on the unusual concentration of global advantage. Add in special factors, such as British expropriation of India's cotton industry through imports of raw cotton and laws taxing India's manufactured wares, and Western industrialization was off and running. Western industrialization was based on global economic power relationships, and it allowed the industrial West to increase the exploitation of other parts of the world, spurring poverty, even as its own wealth expanded. No further explanation may be needed.

Approach 2

There were internal factors in the industrial revolution (though global elements played a role as well), but they were impersonal, happening in the West but not involving features that really defined Western civilization. Anonymous forces that combined to push industrialization included growing market opportunities, thanks to the expansion of overseas trade but also to the new levels of consumerism at home. Improved investment capital facilitated new business behavior, again without any particular input from Western values or institutions. Finally, Europe's population began to expand rapidly, thanks to the impact of newly adopted crops such as the potato. West European population grew 50–100% in the last half of the 18th century. In turn, this forced many rural workers to realize that they could no longer count on access to the land, which compelled them, usually amid great reluctance, to work in unpleasant new factories with noisy and dangerous new equipment. Dramatic population growth also explains business innovation. Jean Schlumberger, in eastern France, was a typical modest manufacturer in the 1760s, content to use established craft methods. But he had 10 children, and none of them died – which was how population expansion affected him personally. To provide for his brood according to conventional middle-class standards, he began to grow his business and haltingly to adopt some of the new textile manufacturing equipment. Soon he was a leading industrialist, though a nervous one, and two of his sons took the process further, becoming really dynamic entrepreneurs in the region. Again, no special Western ideas here, just the driving force of population and its own causes in impersonal developments such as the introduction of the potato.

Approach 3

But there is the third, Western civilization explanation, that can be grafted onto the first two approaches. Population growth, for example, does not automatically stimulate an economic revolution – it had not done so in the West during the Middle Ages when, in fact, a lack of innovation ultimately helped push population levels down; it did not do so in China, where population pressure mounted from about 1650 onward. So even though population growth was undoubtedly involved, it begs for some additional factors – which is where special Western features enter in.

1   Pre-established emphasis on the importance of merchants set a foundation for a newer, risk-taking business spirit. Many individual merchants shied away, preferring the more tested and prestigious concentration on commerce. But some, seeking advancement, launched into new methods from a family basis in the merchant class. Add to this, to help explain some of the difference between the new entrepreneurial spirit and more conventional merchant values, not only population pressure but also the impact of religious change. A disproportionate number of early industrialists were in religious minorities, like Protestants in France or Quakers or evangelicals in Britain. These were people who particularly felt that economic success witnessed God's grace and who also, as minorities, were blocked from normal channels of achievement in government. Finally, the Enlightenment added its push, in justifying material achievement and praising those who could harness nature.

Matthew Bolton, who exploited the first practical steam engine, believed deeply in Enlightenment-style progress. Industrialization may also have been boosted by Enlightenment economists, like Adam Smith, who emphasized the creative force of competition and urged government to be cautious in trying to regulate economic change. Here was a final source of relevant business values.

2   We have seen that the West had increasingly come to value technology and to measure societies by its level. These commitments were enhanced by the earlier evolution of Western manufacturing equipment, which now turned into revolution; and by scientific arguments about how nature could be tamed to the benefit of humankind. James Watt, the inventor of the first fully useful steam engine, had some knowledge of scientific work on gasses and made science equipment for the University of Glasgow. There was a prior basis in the civilization for the extraordinary spurt of technological innovation.

3   Add to the entrepreneurial spirit and commitment to technology the increasing enthusiasm of governments. European governments worked hard to promote industrialization by helping to standardize national trade conditions, encouraging investment banks and stable currency, building or supporting a transportation network including canals and, soon, railroads, and so on. The endeavor tied into two established features of the Western state: first, the tendency toward new functions and rationalization, which had grown fairly steadily during the early modern centuries. And, second, the excitement about any development that might provide an edge in military rivalries, that old Western staple. German governments, for example, were first drawn into railroad development because it would facilitate the movement of troops. The result stimulated heavy industry's growth, but that was not the original intent. Military precedent was also involved in the kind of factory discipline that quickly developed, another connection worth noting.

It is hard to avoid the conclusion that some distinctive Western trends and values provided the final push that set the industrial wheel in motion. They would not have worked without contributions from global and impersonal forces, but there was a link to the Western past. Industrialization's location was no accident.

Furthermore, whatever mix of causes works best to explain this huge transformation, Westerners have long believed that distinctive aspects of their civilization do provide the essential basis for industrialization. On the strength of this belief, Western leaders and observers have frequently told other societies what they need to do – i.e. become more like the West culturally and politically – if they have any hope for industrial success. They criticized other societies for falling short of Western qualities in the 19th century, and they have been doing it again in recent decades – which does not always endear the West to other societies.

One final point: though Western qualities may have been crucial to the first industrial revolution, they have not in fact proved indispensable once the model was established, open to imitation. Other societies had to copy Western technology and science, and they usually imitated some government procedures, including mass education, that the West established during its own industrial century. But they did not need to replicate a Western-style entrepreneurial spirit. It turned out in Japan, for example, that modified Confucian values, promoting group cooperation and tight government–business links, worked quite well – at some points, perhaps better than freewheeling Western individualism. This kind of complication to the West's position in the expanding industrial world becomes a significant issue in 20th century history.

Industrialization's consequences and Western identity

Just as it flowed in part from Western themes, so the industrial revolution enhanced some of them. But, as befits a revolutionary change, industrialization also added to the definition of Westernness. And finally, it raised two kinds of new problems for the West's self-definition.

Industrialization extended a Western commitment to using technology as a measure of social progress. The impulse to deplore other societies as backward because they lagged behind Western industrialization represented a further step is what was already a well-established impulse. Joining technology now was a greater commitment to science, seen as capable not only of unlocking nature's secrets, but also of contributing actively to technical advance and also to achievements in medicine and public health. Here was another way to celebrate Western progress and lament the superstitions of other peoples. Finally, industrialization on the whole undercut the place of religion in Western life, though this was truer in Western Europe than in the United States. Many European workers abandoned religious practice, and even the middle classes tended to spend more time on material enjoyments than on church activities. Ironically, the 19th century saw greatly increased missionary activity in other parts of the world, fueled in part by industrial prosperity; but within the West, secular commitments gained ground.

Industrialization also promoted many of the family values that had been germinating during the early modern centuries. The economic functions of families declined with industrialization, particularly as work moved outside the home and as childhood became increasingly devoted to schooling rather productive labor. Huge adjustments were necessary, including the rapid reduction of the birth rate, as a response to the new economic costs that children posed. But, headed by the growing middle class, most Westerners responded by increasing the idealization of family life and its emotional rewards. Children were seen as innocents to be protected and enjoyed, though grudging child labor restrictions only slowly extended this vision to the working class. Women were hailed as domestic angels, providing beauty and moral guidance to family life. At least in principle, though certainly not always in reality, the Western home began to be seen as a "haven in a heartless world." New products were sold on grounds that they would embellish home and family life. Again, judgments of other societies increasingly reflected Western views about the qualities of their family life when measured against the enhanced Western standards. In turn, visitors from other societies were often startled by Western family patterns. Japanese emissaries in the 1860s noted the respect given women, and their power within the family; the priorities seemed strange, for, as one observer noted, women were given a prestige that should properly be accorded to the family elders.

Besides intensifying some established Western values, industrialization began to encourage some new ones. Industrial conditions prompted an upheaval in the arts, particularly the visual arts, by the end of the 19th century. New materials encouraged new building styles, including the skyscraper (an American invention). Partly because of the impact of photography, partly because of an alienation from industrial life, many artists began experimenting with radical new painting styles, moving toward steadily greater abstraction. While popular taste often continued to prefer older forms, leading artists often explicitly renounced Western artistic traditions in favor of what became known as "modern art." Some of the same innovative spirit spilled over into literature and music. Again, there was resistance. Key conservative movements within the West (later including fascism and Nazism) rejected modern art. Communist Russia did the same, viewing it as a sign of Western decadence. The trends nevertheless continued, as the West became associated with unprecedented artistic experimentation, an identity that persists today.

Still more important was the growing link between Western civilization and consumerism. The growing profusion of factory production pressed for new levels of consumption. So did the nature of industrial work and family life. Many people, particularly in the working classes, but also among sales-clerks and other middle-class ranks, found industrial work increasingly stressful and boring. Working days were squeezed by a rapid pace and precise, clock-based timing under the eyes of unforgiving supervisors. Skill levels and a sense of creativity declined. In this situation, many people adjusted by seeking a better life off the job. And as wages began to advance, and work time declined, this better life was increasingly defined in terms of consumer standards. New items of clothing and home furnishings – including, for middle-class folk, the ubiquitous piano – were joined by brand new products like bicycles. This kind of consumerism meant that many Westerners were defining their lives increasingly in terms of the process and results of acquisition. Shopping in luxurious department stores became a major activity.

Consumerism spilled over into other leisure pursuits, as Western life was increasingly defined by a daily alternation between work and recreation. Commercial leisure, by the later 19th century, meant primarily paying for something to watch – either sports or music hall or, soon, movies. Professional sports as well as amateur competitions spread widely, headed by European soccer and American baseball.

Western civilization, viewed both from inside and from without, became increasingly known in terms of consumer levels and consumer fashions. Here, clearly, was industrialization's most important addition to the definition of the West.

Finally, industrialization explicitly complicated two established aspects of Western culture and political values. In power terms, industrialization promoted authoritarianism, in the factory if not in the state itself. More and more workers found their daily lives shaped by bosses and by detailed factory rules that governed the use of time, prohibited activities like singing or socializing on the job, and even sought to regulate emotion – as when sales-clerks were told to smile whatever the customer provocation. By 1900 the United States was leading in a movement to give new power to industrial engineers to regulate workers' motions and to defy trade union protest. Workers often struggled for greater workplace democracy, but they never, at least before the 21st century, got very far. Even middle-class workers, as corporate bureaucracies replaced individual entrepreneurs, found themselves hemmed in by new regulations and supervisory procedures.

Formal political arrangements might compensate at least in part, as parliaments and voting rights became more common in Western societies. But there was a new dichotomy between official Western political values, which emphasized controls over authority and opportunities for political expression, and what was happening in daily life. The growth of social unrest and class conflict in Western society – including the United States, where strike movements proliferated from the later 19th century through the 1950s – reflected this important tension. And it was also true that governments themselves took on new functions, regulating housing and public health, requiring education, providing more extensive police forces. World War I would reveal how extensively governments could control economic and social life, when the powers of the industrial state were bent to mass mobilization.

Industrialization also contradicted individualism, to the extent that this had become a Western trademark. Industrial work was faceless and regimented. Consumer products were widely standardized. Schools helped teach Western children to learn in the same ways, according to the same clock. The Western commitment to individualism persisted in principle. During the 19th century, for example, the custom of celebrating birthdays spread widely, as a means of helping children recognize their own identity. Modern art might allow some people – beginning with the artists themselves – to gain more individualistic expression. But here, too, there was a new tension within Western life.

There was also a final issue, just beginning to emerge around 1900. Initially, industrialization greatly expanded the West's power in the world, undergirding the final explosion of imperialism. To many outside the West, Western civilization became associated with raw assertions of power and little else. But the same process encouraged other societies to begin to copy more aspects of the West, sometimes including industrialization itself. Japan and Russia, in particular, began their own industrial revolutions by 1900. They also copied other aspects of the contemporary West, such as mass education and a growing focus on science. And they imported elements of Western consumerism, including modern sports: Japanese schoolboys, as early as the 1890s, scored a baseball victory over a team of US sailors, to the nation's great delight. But here was a new question: if non-Western societies could industrialize, could build cities according to Western urban styles, and could even field competitive sports teams – were they Western? Was the West definably different? If Western civilization meant, increasingly, consumerism, science, secularism, and industrial forms of work, all of which some other regions could successfully copy; and if being Western now depended on claiming unchallenged world supremacy – the answers might be unsettling.

In 1900, this final question was just emerging, for no clearly non-Western society was yet an industrial equal – though this depended on assuming the upstart United States was Western, which not all Europeans were sure about. But as Western leaders began to talk of a looming "Yellow Peril," given stirrings in Japan and even China, there was a sense that Western position, if not identity, were going to be challenged. Questions would deepen during the 20th century.

Further reading

Peter N. Stearns, *The Industrial Revolution in World History* (Boulder, Colo.: Westview Press, 1993); Joel Mokyr, *The British Industrial Revolution: An Economic Perspective* (Boulder: Westview Press, 1993); Peter N. Stearns and Henrick Chapman, *European Society in Upheaval: A Social History Since 1750* (London: Macmillan, 1992).

Chapter 11

Disruptions of the twentieth century

To many Western observers, the 20th century started out brightly enough. Newspaper commentary, on the turn of the century, looked back on the 19th century and found it good, in current Western terms. Knowledge had advanced, science and material standards had gained, political rights had expanded. And, of course, through imperialism the West was providing needed guidance to the rest of the world, though there was some uncertainty about whether this stewardship was temporary – that is, that other peoples could become civilized in Western terms – or a permanent responsibility. Warnings about new threats to imperial hegemony qualified a few commentaries, but in general optimism prevailed. A whole school of history had developed – called Whiggish, after a nickname for English middle-class liberals – that saw the past as a great seedbed of Western values, with each major stage moving closer to current Western perfection. This was the outlook, indeed, that helped generate the Western civ course in the United States, under the ministrations of James Robinson and others.

Thirty years later this view was hard to come by, particularly outside the United States. Warnings of the decline of the West, along something like Roman imperial lines, circulated widely, pushed by the German historian Oswald Spengler. World War I had been a massive bloodletting within the West, though with larger global implications. Fascism and Nazism were gaining strength, raising new questions about the definition and validity of Western civilization. Some observers wondered whether Western values were compatible with advanced industrial societies and mass culture. Threats from outside the West, from the Soviet Union and Japan and from the gathering forces of anticolonialism, added to the confusion. Small wonder that many self-appointed defenders of Western values wished that the 20th century had not happened, or that the United States broke ranks with its Western allies and retreated to diplomatic isolationism.

In the longer run, the 20th century saw the West revive; the century clearly must be broken into two major chunks, in Western civ terms. But there are significant analytical issues attached to both chunks, as this chapter explores first a horror and then a surprising rebirth.

Crisis and redefinition

World War I began the downward spiral. It seemed initially to fit within the Western tradition. Western nations had often gone to war. Loyalty to the nation-state, increasing in fervor during the late 19th century, added to the impulse. Some historians have even argued that, because of the lack of significant war in the West for several decades, many young men, and their adult leaders, were getting bored, eager for a call to action. Certainly the first troops marched off gaily enough, assuming that quick action would bring victory safely home. Of course the war turned out very differently. The sheer level of slaughter, the frustration of years of stalemated trench warfare, the shock of new and deadly weaponry, all represented challenges to Western assumptions – they would indeed have challenged the assumptions of any civilization. It was hard to explain how things could be so awful. What happened, in effect, was that the power of industrial technology had transformed war and its impact beyond recognition. In the wake of the war, many people, particularly but not exclusively disillusioned veterans, could not believe that Western civilization could ever be put back together.

The war brought other challenges. Societies outside Europe, headed by Japan and the United States, took advantage of the war to make economic gains at Europe's expense. Stirrings in the colonies, against European control, intensified. The Russian Revolution brought another new threat to what many Westerners thought of as their way of life. Finally, the war revealed the new powers that governments could command, again outstripping any Western tradition, indeed any prior political tradition anywhere. Here, too, the war raised questions about the compatibility of the technologies and organizations possible in advanced industrial societies, with Western precedents.

The 1920s brought some claims of normalcy. Parliamentary democracy briefly expanded its hold in countries such as Germany and Italy. New nations of east–central Europe also immediately adopted these forms, but in all cases except Czechoslovakia they quickly failed, replaced by authoritarian states, which dimmed the achievement considerably. Western science, modern art, and consumerism all resumed their march.

The 1920s also confirmed several changes in women's conditions that cumulatively added to the West's distinctiveness and self-definition. There was a precedent earlier, in the changes in male–female relations that resulted from the European-style family, but the markers now were different, implying much wider equality claims. Building on late 19th century expansions of legal protections for women, for example in divorce, and on the unusually vigorous Western feminist movement, several countries now extended the vote to women. Women also gained new opportunities in leisure and new freedom to appear in public. Educational gains also continued, reducing gender inequalities in this sphere, and a growing number of women made their mark in the arts, professions, and even science. Some of these changes were still disputed. Older traditions were still honored, in assumptions, for example, that women were supposed to be particularly careful in their appearance and in the insistence that domestic and childcare responsibilities were disproportionately female. Nevertheless, gender relations constituted another area where Westerners were striking out in new ways, creating new distinctions from most other societies and adding to the definition of Westernness.

But these trends were quickly overshadowed by the twin challenges of economic depression and fascism. The depression, beginning in 1929, caused an unusual degree of hardship, coming on the heels of the dislocations of World War I. The crisis also further sapped confidence in Western political and economic institutions, while casting doubt on the West's economic leadership in the world at large. It proved hard to rebound. In fact, we now know that some very fruitful developments took shape in the 1930s. New industries, such as television, formed in regions like southern England. Dynamic new businessmen took their first career steps, and some of them would reemerge as European leaders after World War II in what proved to be a remarkable renewal of Europe's managerial class. But these developments were beneath the surface in a bleak decade.

For two patterns described the 1930s in the West. First, leading Western democracies seemed to have lost their will. Britain and France, particularly, suffered from inept leadership and a polarization between political extremes. The combination made decisive action difficult, either in response to the depression or in foreign affairs. The United States was more innovative in domestic matters, with a significant expansion of government functions in the New Deal; but it contributed nothing toward resolving increasing diplomatic tensions, mired as the nation was in isolationism. The paralysis was deadly given the other new force, the emergence of a new kind of right-wing movement headed by German Nazism.

The problem of fascism and Nazism

Fascist movements took shape initially in the 1920s, building on new kinds of conservative attacks on modern society before World War I. In some respects, the movements were blatantly antiWestern, despite their popularity in countries that seemed central to the West. They attacked individualism in the name of group loyalty, the state, and a single leader. They blasted parliaments for their political divisions and their constraints on strong government initiatives. They criticized modern consumerism, modern art, and the changes in women's roles, urging a return to real or imagined folk forms and female domesticity and childbearing. Ultimately, fascism, combined with weak response from the remaining democracies, introduced another set of horrors to 20th century Western history, bringing another world war and the unprecedented slaughter of six million Jews, plus many others, in the Nazi Holocaust.

How could this happen in Western civilization? Aside from a head-in-the-sand wish that the 20th century would go away, there have been two principal interpretive responses. The first emphasizes the extent to which the leading fascist countries, and particularly Germany, were not in fact really Western, despite their undeniable participation in many aspects of Western history and numerous contributions, from music to the modern university, to Western life. Nazism, according to this line of argument, springs from Germanness, not Westernness.

A great deal of research went into a search for a German *Sonderweg*, or special way, to explain how a society could go so wrong. All of the *Sonderweg* analysis went beyond the special circumstances Germany faced after 1918, which everyone acknowledges played a key role in spurring Nazism: defeat in war after the government had kept Germans hopeful that victory was near; the fact that the military leadership made a new civilian government take responsibility for the peace settlement, which tainted the regime even though it had not had anything to do with the conduct of war; a terrible price inflation in the early 1920s (for which the government did bear some responsibility, but which really unsettled the middle classes by pounding down the value of savings); a bad peace settlement which stripped Germany of key territory, severely limited the military which made both leaders and veterans all the more disgruntled, and also treated the nation as if it had been solely at fault for the war, imposing heavy reparations which further damaged the economy; and a depression which, partly because of the war's consequences, hit Germany unusually hard after 1919. None of this, according to *Sonderweg* analysis, quite explains why so many Germans could voluntarily fall for such a horrible political movement (at a peak in free elections in 1932, about 37% of all voters picked the Nazis) and then stay largely silent under a regime that became still more horrible as time went on.

Here are the main features of Germany's special historical path, and, of course, they can be combined with each other as well as with the war and postwar dislocation. In politics, the Prussian state had traditionally emphasized strong authority and a large army. Germany had long been disunited, and then between 1864 and 1871 gained unity by war. All of this increased nationalism more than was usual in Europe (so the argument goes) and linked it to militarism and a strong state. National success weakened the middle-class commitment to liberalism, for liberals accepted a fairly weak parliament, including the emperor's appointment of the executive ministers along with limits on the freedom of the press, because they were so excited about unity. When Germany did get full parliamentary institutions after World War I, in the Weimar republic, it did not have a strong enough liberal tradition to provide adequate support. Late unity also caused a pervasive sense that the other great European powers were not giving Germany its due, for example in imperialism, so when the war settlement punished Germany directly resentment was greater than it might otherwise have been. All of which, in turn, made a vigorously authoritarian, militaristic political movement that promised a glorious foreign policy unusually attractive.

Culturally, some have argued that Germans – particularly, Lutheran Germans – had a distinctively internal idea of freedom, which could make them feel free even under an authoritarian state. Again, this points to weak liberalism.

Socially, Germany had an unusually powerful landed aristocracy, the Prussian Junkers, who wanted a state that would maintain their social and economic prestige. Though not for the most part Nazi, they accepted Nazism because it secretly pledged a defense of aristocratic privilege. Under the Junkers, many peasants had long lacked much freedom, which may have made them, too, quick to support a nationalist movement that promised a defense of peasant values against modern life. (Nazis were big on promoting peasant costumes and such.) Germany had industrialized very fast and created a powerful big business class that often allied with the Junkers. Overall, German society had not kept pace with its economy. One result, besides traditionalist peasants, was a large artisan and shopkeeper class that resented modern economic forms, like the department store, which threatened growing competition; again, Nazism, which promised to restore artisan guilds though it largely broke its promise in favor of promoting big business and a war economy, could seem a solution to a society under systematic stress even before World War I. Germany's social structure was simply less flexible than France's or England's, and rapid industrialization was all the more disruptive.

And so Germany was not really Western, which makes a clearly anti-Western political movement and regime unsurprising without calling Western civilization directly into account. The Western nations are still responsible for their timid, sluggish response to Nazism, until World War II forced their hand, but at least Nazism itself is not laid at the Western door. There are a few holes in the *Sonderweg* analysis: notably, Prussia, where strong government and weak peasants had their greatest hold, was not a hotbed of Nazism compared, for example, to Catholic regions such as Bavaria. But lots of really thoughtful scholars, German and non-German, have poured great intelligence and historical insight into the search for a special explanation.

But *Sonderweg* analysis has declined in popularity in recent years, mainly, of course, because Germany now seems thoroughly Western and the pressure of explaining Nazism and its atrocities is far less acute. (Historical thinking is always susceptible to the impact of current conditions, and this is one of the factors involved here; the *Sonderweg* interest may have dropped more than it should as a result.) Far more work now sees Germany's history as fairly similar to that of its neighbors, its social structure, for example, quite comparable to that of France. But this might mean, of course, that Nazism has more to do with the West than some observers might wish.

While Nazism was unusually powerful and awful, strong fascist, anti-Jewish movements cropped up in many parts of the West after World War I – particularly, of course, in Italy (though the anti-Jewish part came only later) and France. Fascism did not win out in France but fascistic movements sometimes had as many as two million supporters; and France's wartime regime, though partly imposed by the Germans after the French defeat, had fascist elements. Spain also picked up fascism, though partly on the strength of German example. To be sure, fascism was weak in Britain, Scandinavia, and the settler societies including the United States, where among other things the parliamentary tradition was unusually strong. But maybe it was in fact Western, and not simply a German aberration.

And here is how this possibility might play out. Fascism was antiWestern in many ways but it highlighted several Western features, taking them out of full context. Notably, it emphasized a strong state as absolutism had done, though going much further in part because, with industrialization and the World War I example, governments could be much more powerful than absolutists had ever imagined save in rhetoric. Fascism strongly played up fervent nationalism, which was a Western creation. It built on a tradition of anti-Semitism that went back to the Middle Ages. And a fascination with military virtues and military competitions was as old as the West itself, and all the fascist movements played on this tradition. So a real Western component was there.

Then, fascism also built on the shock of World War I and a wider sense that industrial society needed to be brought under greater control, to protect older values and social groups. Germany was not alone here. Many sectors – the military, the aristocracy, and in places like Spain the church – were willing to use new, desperate measures to preserve their social power, and fascism could suit the bill. Fear of communism added into this mix – and many non-fascist Westerners shared this fear in the 1920s and 1930s.

Germany went to extremes, but this is because of the war and postwar dislocations, and also because of Hitler's particular evil genius, not because Germany was nonWestern. Other regions moved in similar directions. The West is not off the hook. Even at the time, thoughtful observers, such as the novelist Sinclair Lewis in the United States with his book *It Can't Happen Here*, worried that fascism could spread more widely in the West. Even after World War II fears of revived fascism have troubled not only Germans and Italians, but also French observers and others. No one would argue that fascism was typically Western or some logical outgrowth of Western history; but there may be more link than is sometimes recognized. In extreme circumstances, in other words, the West harbors its own opponents. And while events in the past 50 years have greatly eased fears of fascist recurrence, it may be that the memory not only of the movement, but of its links to Western civilization, is worth maintaining, to warn Westerners of their own dark side.

The postwar West

Defining Western civilization after World War II becomes much easier, and on the whole vastly more pleasant. Partly because of fascist excesses and then their military defeat in war, many Europeans really learned from their recent history, which prompted them, first, to reassert Western values like parliamentarism and protections of individual liberty and, second, to redefine a few features of the West that had undoubtedly contributed to the West's collapse between the wars. Never, since the age of feudalism, had the various nations of the West shared so many roughly similar political institutions, based now on democratic, parliamentary regimes and constitutional protections of individual rights.

And several key Western nations combined their unexpected resurgence with an ability to handle their rapid loss of empire. Britain, the United States, Holland, and, more grudgingly, France all accepted the decolonization movement – not without regret, not without some vicious rearguard action in some places. Overall, both leaders and ordinary people agreed that domestic stability was more important than defense of empire at all costs; and the defense probably would have failed in any events, as France learned first in Vietnam, then in Algeria. Portugal accepted the same lessons in the 1970s.

Decolonization was cushioned by the fact Europe retained great economic and cultural power in many former colonies, but the fact remains it was a big change that could have overwhelmed the West – but did not. Nor did the Cold War turn out to derail a considerable Western revival. The United States emerged as the leading military power, overshadowing Western Europe, and this was a significant shift. Cold War rivalries may have helped solidify Western unity against the presumed communist threat; certainly it helped spur Marshall plan aid and some of the first steps toward European unity.

Three other major changes contrasted the postwar period with its predecessor, in terms of Western civilization. First, with the careful establishment of parliamentary democracies in West Germany and Italy, and the revivification of democratic government in France, the West was redefined in terms of a commitment to multiparty democracy (including, now, women's suffrage everywhere save Switzerland, which delayed until the 1970s), and considerable protection of freedoms of speech and religion. Fascism was gone, save as a minority political impulse that cropped up occasionally. Second, after an agonizing period of postwar disruption, rapid economic growth returned to Western Europe. Germany's "economic miracle" of the 1950s returned it to the ranks of industrial giants. Equally striking were rapid growth gains in France and Italy. With prosperity, consumerist patterns resumed with a vengeance, in the form of standard household items such as refrigerators and televisions, growing ownership of automobiles, and growing use of commercial leisure forms. Social tensions eased considerably, compared to the interwar period. In the context of an expanding economy women began to enter the formal labor force in increasing numbers, a significant addition to their position in Western society. With all this, scientific research and innovations in modern art persisted as well, additional talismans of Western identity.

The third major change, within Europe though with United States encouragement, involved a significant reduction of nationalist emphasis and militarism, beginning in the 1950s. Old enmities between France and Germany were officially buried. Multinational European administrations, ultimately embodied in the Common Market (later called the European Union), provided successful cooperation across national lines. Military commitments continued, though Germany was constrained. But civilian budgets grew faster, particularly once Europe became resigned to decolonization and American military protections. In the 1980s a German politician hailed Western Europe as the first modern example of "civil societies," in which military goals no longer played a significant role in the definition of political success. Here were significant alterations in the West's traditional self-definition, assuming they persisted.

Not everything was roses, of course. Economic growth sometimes faltered. There were new discontents. A new round of feminism in the 1970s contended that gains for women had not gone far enough. Youth unrest in the 1960s targeted the sterility of a consumer society, though tensions here eased by the 1970s. Environmentalism, and a strong Green movement in several countries, pointed to a set of pressing issues. Poverty persisted, particularly among immigrant populations – a point we will return to in the next chapter. And many parts of the world resented the West and what it saw as continued arbitrary exercises of power and interference, another aspect of globalization which we will take up later. Even the memories of prior collapse could intrude: if serious problems occurred, there was no guarantee that some aberration like fascism might not be a response.

But for all this, the West seemed noticeably healthier and more clearly definable in 2003 than it had been in 1940.

Geography again

One final question concerned the West's revival: the issue of geographical definition and coherence. The zone of a clearly identifiable West expanded within Europe. The decisions, in Spain, Portugal, and Greece to turn to democratic, parliamentary forms in the 1970s were noteworthy. They accompanied membership in the Common Market and more rapid industrial development. Southern Europe remained poorer than the European average, but social changes, including conditions for women and expansion of secular culture, were shifting in common directions. Ireland, long a bit distant because of British colonial control, unusually fervent Catholicism, and poverty, also moved toward more core European characteristics, as did Finland. The European frontiers of the West were integrating.

The same process would probably occur for east–central Europe in the early 21st century, given the collapse of the Soviet system. Poland, the Czech Republic, the Baltic states, Hungary, Slovenia, and the Slovak Republic all moved toward market-based economies and a seemingly firm multiparty democracy. All, also, sought European Union membership. (Eastern Germany integrated directly with West Germany, and while tensions remained presumably this, too, betokened Westernism, based on deep East German interests in greater political freedom and access to Western consumer standards.) Unusual poverty remained in east–central Europe, and there were other alignment issues, but fuller integration with Western characteristics seemed likely. The situation was less clear for the rest of the Balkans. In Serbia, the legacy of ethnic rivalry and internal warfare in the 1990s had not yet been remedied. Bulgaria and Romania were less clearly committed to multi-party democracy. But possibilities for further change remained. The West might expand some more. And the question of Russia's new relationship with the West remained open as well.

The inclusion of the United States and Western Europe in a common Western civilization raised some unexpected new issues. In many ways Western Europe and the United States converged further in the 20th century, and particularly after World War II. The war and economic change finally destroyed the European aristocracy as a significant social force. The peasantry shrank, and those who remained turned to commercial agriculture. The European countryside lacked American-style agribusiness, but it was less different than had been the case in the 19th century. Continued economic change and consumer gains reduced urban differences as well. The two regions shared many consumer products, despite some European concern with undue Americanization; by the 1980s, 25% of all restaurants in France were fast-food, many in American chains, much to everyone's surprise given the nation's gourmet reputation. Political extremes in Europe receded with prosperity, and while a socialist tradition persisted many parties dropped older slogans in favor of a more accommodationist position, rather like some sectors of the Democratic party in the United States. The racial divide between the two regions narrowed a bit as Western Europe acquired more immigrants of color and some racial and civil rights issues in consequence, even as reform legislation in the United States weakened the color divide somewhat. Both societies, by 2000, had a substantial minority of racially distinctive people who were also unusually poor, frequently with high unemployment rates.

Another revealing convergence was more personal: In an important shift, European child-rearing became more flexible, less stiff and authoritarian from the late 1950s onward. In this it paralleled changes in American child-rearing that had occurred in the 1920s. The United States was still a bit more permissive with teenagers than Europeans were, a bit more tolerant of a youth consumer culture, but again, the gap had narrowed considerably.

But there were distinctions even so, and some of them widened. The United States had never developed the kind of protective welfare state that Western Europe created by the 1950s, and by the 1980s and 1990s it cut its welfare measures back, under pressure from conservatives plus new-style moderate Democrats. American devotion to free enterprise was matched by Britain, but not the rest of Europe. Europeans were more committed to cushioning the effects of untrammeled capitalism. On a related note: while income inequalities grew within each region at the end of the 20th century, they were much greater in the United States, where a new class of superrich deployed its taste for luxury. An even more important divide opened over leisure. West Europeans sought increasing opportunities for leisure as part of their new-found prosperity. Vacation time expanded rapidly, with many people enjoying 4–6 weeks a year. Not so Americans, where work time actually went up in the 1980s and 1990s. Americans seemed more ensnared by a traditional, 19th century style work ethic – or they were forced into it by the sluggish growth of real wages for the majority of workers. Americans were also more moralistic than Europeans, an offshoot of their greater religiosity. Both regions saw a revolution in teenage sexual behavior in the 1960s, with more, and younger, premarital sex. But Europe responded by extending birth control devices, which quickly cut the teenage pregnancy rate. Americans, hesitant about this kind of encouragement to immorality, resisted, pumping money instead into just-say-no abstinence programs; and despite modest success with abstinence, the American teenage pregnancy rate remained much higher as a result. Moralism showed on the average beach, where Europeans eagerly indulged in topless sunbathing for women as Americans kept the wraps on. On another issue: Western Europe formally renounced the death penalty in the postwar decades, just as most American states loudly revived it.

The greatest gap, indeed an outright role reversal, involved militarism and nationalism. Military spending soared in the United States during the Cold War and even in the 1990s, vastly outstripping the totals of all European nations combined. The size and influence of the military expanded apace, as the nation cast off its traditions of aversion to a large standing force in peace-time. Europe, as we have seen, was moving in the opposite direction. The result showed in power terms: the United States dwarfed Western Europe in military might and corresponding international clout. It showed also in the funds available for non-military spending, for example on urban amenities or welfare (or, indeed, paid vacations), where the reverse held true. It showed, finally, in foreign policy debates, where Europeans were less eager to assert military force over diplomacy, worrying about American aggressiveness and unilateralism, and where Americans frequently found European hesitancy a pain. American nationalism, finally, remained sharper, with far fewer signs of compromise than in the new, transnational Europe.

Disagreements crested, at least briefly, in 2003, when the United States and Britain went to war against Iraq. Several other European countries supported the move, but France, Germany and Belgium held back, and European public opinion, even in Britain, blasted American belligerence. In turn, American leaders lamented the timidity of what they called the "old" Europe. Was this the beginning of a new division of global goals within the West?

Debate about a transatlantic Western civilization was not new, as we have seen. The obvious point is that the terms of the debate changed in the later 20th century, and that prospects for future coherence were not entirely clear. Indices pointed vigorously in both directions. The United States saw itself as the new leader of Western civilization (partly because so many leaders had taken Western civ courses), but the homeland of the West, in Europe, was not sure it agreed on what "Western" now involved. Debate could not easily be resolved, but its existence, and the future directions it implied, remained crucial to calculating where Western civilization stood at the dawn of the 21st century – after a 20th century that many were delighted to shake off.

Further reading

Karl D. Bracher, *The German Dictatorship: The Origins, Structure and Effects of National Socialism* (New York: Praeger Publishers, 1970); Erich Fromm, *Escape From Freedom* (New York: Farrar & Rinehart, 1941); Walter Laqueur, *Fascism Past, Present and Future* (1996); Peter N. Stearns and Herridick Chapman, *European Society in Upheaval: A Social History Since 1750* (London: Macmillan,1992); Walter Laqueur, *Europe in Our Time: A History, 1945–1972* (New York: Viking, 1992). For a comparison of Western democracies in the recent past, Robert Dahl, *How Democratic is the American Constitution?* (New Haven: Yale University Press, 2001).

Chapter 12

The West in a globalized world

As the 21st century opened, the big news in world history was the acceleration of the process called globalization. This chapter takes up key issues about the West and globalization, which means we focus particularly on the last 30 years or so but with some glances back another century before. Globalization raises analytical challenges for any civilization tradition: will peculiarities and distinctive customs fall away before homogeneous global processes? It is appropriate to ask these questions about the West just as we do about Japan or India, for it gets to the heart of a central orientation toward the world's future: can or should separate civilizations survive the unprecedented intensity of international contacts? For the West, patterns of globalization to date also raise questions about power. Globalization thus far has reflected disproportionate West influence; what would happen to the process, and the West's reaction to it, if the Western piece declined?

We begin with a definition. Globalization involves an intensification of the speed, volume, and range of interregional contacts, with growing impact on various aspects of social and individual life. The term emerged in the 1990s, when technologies such as the Internet highlighted a revolutionary potential for new kinds of linkages around the world. Globalization has particularly involved economic linkages (including their environmental impacts), with rapidly growing world trade and the wide-ranging activities of the multinational corporations, and cultural contacts, revolving mainly around international consumerism and media access. Political globalization – the formation of global mechanisms to monitor issues and provide opportunities for expression about global developments – has lagged in contrast.

A false start

Historians have recently pointed out that a first round of globalization occurred in the decades around 1900. Completion of the Suez and then Panama canals accelerated shipping, while transoceanic cables allowed quick telegraph communication around the world. By the 1880s many farmers in India timed their harvests according to market news from the Grain Exchange in Chicago. Legal constraints on shipping goods or moving people internationally were actually lower than they are today. A kind of cultural globalization emerged as well, as region after region copied British or, less commonly, American sports. Then, by the second decade of the 20th century, Hollywood emerged as the movie capital of the world, commanding 65–95% of national markets from the Middle East to Australia and Latin America.

But this first round of globalization failed. Many countries pulled out of the global system, in whole or in part. The United States adopted isolationism, though it continued to participate in the global economy. The Soviet Union, particularly under Stalin, withdrew from the economy, in favor of "socialism in one country," proving at least for a time that a big country could industrialize on its own. Nazi Germany reduced its global economic effort also, and its cultural ties, in favor of creating a separate Nazi culture and a war machine. Japan tried to set up its own Asian Co-Prosperity system, largely through conquest. Later, communist China would also pull out for a while.

The middle decades of the 20th century were littered with signs of the failure of the first round of globalization. There were two, related causes. First, globalization could not survive world war and world depression; the events overwhelmed it. But second, the Western world, and particularly Western Europe, had assumed that what we now call globalization could be run without most of the globe, with decisions taken, imperialist fashion, in the board rooms and ministries of the West. Want to set up an International Postal Union, in the 1870s? Discuss it among the European states with the generous inclusion of the United States, and the system (very valuable to international contacts) was off and running. Want to create a latter-day Olympic games (in the 1890s), arguing for international harmony through sports? Assume again a European–US collaboration, and leave it at that. The same kind of myopia governed the formation of the League of Nations after World War I, which was largely a club for the states of Europe. Small wonder that key regions felt they had no stake in the process, and pulled away as soon as they could. The experiments were important, and some, such as the Olympics, have survived to take on more genuinely global shape in the decades after World War II. But the larger process was stillborn.

In fact, the big news from the middle decades of the 20th century seemed to highlight the decline of the West's relative power in the world at large – even after the West internally began to show signs of revival. The relative power loss followed from a number of key developments. Decolonization was one. The West's direct political control over key parts of the world, which had expanded recurrently from the 15th century onward, now began to draw to a close. Nor, on a related point, did the West retain the easy military advantage it had built up over the same time period. Thanks to new forms of warfare, notably guerrilla tactics, plus the ability of medium-sized states like Iraq to acquire enough weaponry to deter easy attack, marching into parts of Asia or even Africa with 200-man forces that could outgun the natives was a thing of the past by the second half of the 20th century. In key regions, the military power of countries such as India and China involved even greater power shifts. The West continued to have the most potent single military arsenal, with the United States in the lead, particularly once the Soviet Union collapsed. By the 1990s, it also monopolized primary power in the air. But its comparative military advantage, and with this its comparative freedom of action had shrunk quite noticeably. This relative decline involved Western Europe most fully, but even the United States could not easily rival the kind of power that Britain had wielded in the later 19th century, save where airpower alone would suffice. And in the economy, where the West held up better, world position increasingly had to be shared with Japan and the Pacific Rim.

Globalization returns

Yet, despite a previous failure and despite complex power shifts, the process of globalization began to seize center stage again at the end of the 20th century, and, to most observers, it reflected massive Western control and influence. What was going on?

Three factors intertwined. High economic growth rates, particularly in Western Europe and the Pacific Rim, both regions heavily involved in international trade, convinced other regions that participation in the world economy and greater commitment to market forces, rather than a state-run economic policy, constituted keys to success. By the 1970s, many Latin American countries were reducing government controls in favor of a freer market economy. Chile, for example, gained ground in the commercial production of fruits and vegetables for the North American market. During the 1990s, rapid economic growth in the United States, fueled by the high-tech sector, seemed to strengthen the importance of confirming the commitment to international economic participation. American leaders were not bashful in urging other countries to follow the American recipe for prosperity.

Closely related to the importance of the West and the Pacific Rim as models were the growing signs of sluggishness in the largest state-run economies. China made the historic decision, in 1978, to encourage freer economic competition internally and to begin to participate actively in international trade – while retaining a communist political regime. The decision paid off, as China soon began to enjoy 10% annual growth in its gross national product. In the mid-1980s, the Soviet Union, under Mikail Gorbachev, made a similar decision, based on the growing signs of economic collapse amid slow growth and the crushing expenses of military competition with the United States. Gradually, the Soviet economy began to reorganize toward a greater market role, and international participation grew apace. Other countries in the former Soviet bloc converted their economies as well, often more quickly than the Russian giant.

Finally, there was the new round of revolutionary technology. Joining the increasingly dense network of air travel and transport were communications satellites and, soon, the Internet. It was almost impossible to isolate a region from the new bombardment of satellite-transmitted television and computer linkages. (Only a few small countries, such as North Korea and Myanmar, even attempted isolation in this new flurry.) Regions already involved in globalization, including the West, found that connections greatly expanded. International gatherings of all sorts confirmed the process. Scientists and social scientists could meet, in person or virtually, to confirm that their commitments transcended cultural boundaries. The same applied to many business people, often avidly pursuing the same organizational fads. And to athletes: sports competitions still roused nationalist loyalties, but for many athletes the commitment to the game was what mattered, and many players moved easily from team to team across national boundaries.

The globalization of the late 20th century was measurably different from what had gone before. Levels of international trade were 15 times higher than in 1900. Cultural interpenetration was vastly greater: people could and did now watch the same television shows the world over – the American *Baywatch* for a time was the world's most popular production. And a quarter of the world's population might simultaneously watch the same sports competition, such as World Cup football. Multinational corporations were different from earlier international companies. In 1900, important companies traded all over the world and some might set up branch factories to take advantage of local markets. But the true multinational used the world as the production stage, manufacturing parts of products in a dozen different countries, on possibly four continents, to take advantage of lowest labor costs, most favorable environmental laws, and local raw materials. Global environmental issues were unprecedented also. In 1900 a plantation owner in Brazil might introduce rubber trees to a region where they were not native, in hopes of producing for international export, and the result could be serious regional damage to the ecology, for example through erosion. In 2000, an international company, eager to increase beef production, might sponsor the destruction thousands of acres of Brazilian rainforest, not only changing the regional ecology but contributing literally to global climate change. The same boundary-less environmental impact applied to the acid rain caused by airborn transmission of industrial pollutants. The world, as the saying went, was truly getting smaller. There was even concern that, amid all this change, the international transmission of obscure diseases might accelerate, though this remained more a threat than a reality with the major exception of the rapidly spreading AIDS epidemic.

The West's role

The new round of globalization involved a mixture of change and continuity where the West was concerned, again in comparison to a century before.

Change seemed to predominate in the politics of globalization. Though the United Nations Security Council reflected Western dominance, with three of five permanent seats, each with veto power, designated for Western countries, the UN as a whole expanded to a full global array. Relatedly, UN sponsored conferences, whether on women, or birth control, or environmental protection, had a similarly global cast of characters. Other international bodies, such as the Olympics committee, similarly shed most of their older Western leanings. One result, of course, was that votes might go against Western wishes, which roused some opposition particularly in the United States, against a United Nations which was no longer a predictable pawn.

There were two limitations, however, to the globalization of politics. First, as noted above, global politics did not keep pace with the other aspects of globalization. Controls over environmental impact, for example, fell well short of the rate of degradation, in the eyes of many observers. Many international agreements depended on the willingness of nations or even of multinational companies (which were more powerful than many nations) to enforce, and the record here was spotty. Second, the West preserved disproportionate influence in some aspects of global politics – despite genuine change in the composition of international bodies. The continued military and particularly economic power of the West made it first among equals in many respects. It was hard to imagine, for example, a genuinely global decision about pollution that would not give special weight to the views of the West and Japan – simply because they held the funds that would go into any remedial effort. The imbalance was starker where outright economic policies were concerned. Agencies like the World Bank and the International Monetary Fund, making decisions about development loans, were dominated by the West plus Japan. Annually, the heads of the six top Western powers, plus Japan, and recently as a courtesy Russia, met to ponder global economic policy. And, even where economic issues were not at the forefront, Western opinion seemed to have special impact. United Nations conferences on women, for example, frequently reflected the views of Western feminists to a surprising extent. Western confidence that its standards were the most appropriate, the power of the Western media, the sense on the part of many regions that a failure to live up to Western norms was somehow a sign of backwardness – an occasion for international embarrassment, all contributed to this tendency. A further result was that, not infrequently, agreements were reached, for example on women's rights to equal property, that national courts would then not enforce because of the contradiction between Western and local standards. Clearly, the scope of global politics and the place of the West and Western values in shaping these politics, were far from resolved.

In the economy, globalization was no longer a Western playpen, as had been largely the case around 1900; but the lead actors were still the West plus Japan and the Pacific Rim. Japan alone had become the second largest industrial producer in the world, after the United States, a tremendous achievement for a relatively small nation with poor natural resources. This addition was significant, but it hardly added up to global equality. Most of the great multinational corporations were Western, Japanese or Korean. Most of the key new global technology stemmed from the same regional sources. The Internet, for example, resulted from US military research on communications enhancement, then popularized and more widely applied, in 1990, by a British engineer working in Switzerland. Other regions now formed part of an active supporting cast; again, the Western global international presence was not as all-consuming as it had been in 1900. India's high-tech sector, China's rapidly expanding exports, Brazil's role as a leading exporter of steel and computers, the special bargaining power of the oil-producing states in the Middle East – these and other developments qualified the gap between dominators and dominated in the global economy.

The fact remained, however, that the global inequalities in income got worse, not better, in the last decades of the 20th century. China's huge export surge was extremely impressive, but it was heavily based on low-wage, exploited labor. It was still possible to hope that global participation would pay off more widely. But many reports, for example in 2002, sounded gloomily similar to those of a century before: hourly wages in the textile industry in Turkey, Pakistan, and Mexico were going down despite increasing exports to the United States; banana workers in the Andes went on strike because of a 25% pay cut due to falling prices and overproduction; several global firms left Mexico for China or Vietnam because Mexican wages had moved up from the bargain basement. Again, it remained significant that the West was no longer the only beneficiary from economic globalization. Low-wage textile operations in South Africa and Lesotho were as often Korean as Western; and in some cases Western firms were rated as slightly fairer and more generous employers than strictly local operations were. But no one could argue that globalization had yet unlocked the secret of general benefit, and to many observers the West seemed suspiciously profiteering.

Indeed, from 2000 onward a series of protests against globalization began to take place at the meetings of agencies such as the World Bank. Protesters included trade unionists from Western nations worried about losing jobs to low-wage competition; environmentalists concerned about deteriorating environmental quality amid the ceaseless pressure to produce, representatives from poorer nations concerned about the squeeze on wages, and various protesters opposed to the threats to regional cultural identity posed by global commerce. The protests were ineffective, and it was not clear how economic globalization could successfully be resisted. But it was clear that not all was well in this central pillar of globalization, and that much of the blame fell on the West.

Finally, cultural globalization, even more purely than economic, was Western through and through. There were a few minor qualifications. Japanese media enjoyed some global success. Many animated films shown worldwide came from Japan. For a time in the 1990s a leading female role model in Iran was a character in a Japanese-made animated television series. Japanese and Taiwanese rock stars gained fame in Korea and China. And a whole variety of nations broke through to international leadership in key sports areas, even though most of the games were of Western origin. The 2002 World Cup quarterfinals thus included teams from East Asia and Africa for the first time, while Olympic gold became increasingly widely shared particularly with China's push into bigtime international sports.

But the definers of popular music, television, and film were Western. The spread of fast foods derived solely from the West, primarily the United States – with only minor regional adjustments such as more vegetarian fare in India or teriyaki in Japan. Disney products and Western dolls like Barbie, either directly or in imitations, increasingly inspired children's toys around the world. Western-style celebrations gained ground, for example Christmas shopping in Muslim Turkey, or American-derived Halloween trick-or-treating in northern Mexico on what had once been a sacred holiday. Some of the most expensive Western consumer creations, such as Disney theme parks, could only be afforded in wealthy societies; a Disney park did gangbuster business in Japan. But the spread of Western fashions, including blue jeans and revealing clothing for adolescent girls, easily surmounted cultural and financial barriers, contributing to something like a global youth culture. Even Western body types, and specifically the emphasis on slenderness for girls and women, spread to other societies along with the more conventional media influence. Western tourism created other inroads, with resorts featuring Western habits, including topless sunbathing, from Malaysia to the Caribbean.

Even as Western power declined, and as economic leadership was shared with the Pacific Rim, there was simply no global rival to Western popular culture and particularly to Western consumerism. The only way to break through to more than regional cultural impact seemed to involve taking on Western trappings. This was true for Japanese rock stars; it was true for Indian movies, which set up a Hollywood-like operation in Bombay, called Bollywood, that blended Indian themes with Hollywood glitz and won some international success by the early 21st century. People sought Western outlets even when they did not particularly like them, simply because it gave them a sense of being in fashion, of participating in something larger than the local. Thus many McDonald's patrons in Hong Kong noted that they really did not care for the food, but they went to see and be seen.

So add it up: this was not unchanged globalization, but observers could be excused for thinking that globalization and Westernization meant almost the same things. The disproportionate influence of Western political standards, in areas such as human rights or women's rights; disproportionate share at the top of the global economy, a position enhanced in the 1990s when Japan's economy faltered somewhat; and virtual monopoly on cultural globalization, with its emphasis on science, secularism, and consumerism – all this added up to an intimidating package.

And the package, in turn, raised two further questions: about the West as target of global attack, and about a global Westernization obscuring the West itself.

The West and the world

The problems of targeting and homogenization were opposed ends of the globalization spectrum. The fact that they can both be legitimately raised shows how complex and uncertain the whole globalization process remains.

Globalization raised understandable concerns about identity, about control – and, of course, about economic outcomes. As globalization advanced it was striking how many regions rose to assert heightened identity claims. Some of these were within the West, as regional movements for greater autonomy and cultural recognition in Scotland, or Britanny, or French Quebec surfaced or gained momentum. A few of these spilled into violence, as with the Basque movement in Spain and France. The collapse of the Soviet system encouraged even more vigorous statements of regional identity in parts of southeastern Europe and central Asia. The impulse could easily be directed against globalization, and against the West as globalization's sponsor.

The rise of religious fundamentalism from the 1970s onward had similar implications. It often drew from impoverished urban groups, left behind or even further exploited by global economic forces. As in the Iranian revolution of 1979, it frequently targeted the habits of a Western-influenced consumer society and the activities of Western tourists and business people that offended religious prescriptions. Frequently, Westernizing elements within the region were the most direct focus of the religious leaders; this was the case, for example, with Hindu fundamentalism in India. But again, the West could be directly cited as well. Middle-Eastern terrorism, which burst out so strikingly in 2001 against the symbols of Western capitalism and military power – the World Trade Center and the Pentagon – had a mix of motives. Hatred of Israel, rejection of the United States military presence in the Persian gulf, dislike of secular authoritarian governments within the Middle East itself – all were involved along with cultural and economic globalization. But globalization entered in strongly, and there was no sign that the tension would soon end.

Despite the decline of imperialism, in other words, the West's role in globalization roused important new hostilities for the West in the world at large. Because of new global links and the flexibility of modern weaponry, these hostilities could be brought home far more directly than had been possible in 1900. Few Westerners argued that globalization should be called off as a result, but there were divisions about an appropriate response, particularly concerning the extent to which military reactions would prove useful. Targeting the West might highlight some Western characteristics like consumerism or a particular take on women's rights; but it also might make the West more defensive, less tolerant.

At the other end of the spectrum, and admittedly on a somewhat more abstract level, some analysts worried that globalization was becoming too successful, in progressively erasing some of the traditions and hallmarks that had defined separate civilizations and, through this, had made the world a home for interesting and creative diversity. Usually this concern applied particularly to non-Western societies whose distinctiveness risked being bulldozed by Westernization. But the issues could be directed toward the West as well: if and as the world becomes Western, would a Western identity be lost? We have seen that one of the impulses for the passionate defense of Western civ courses by the 1990s involved a fear that the West might be overrun by Westernized but not fully Western immigrants or cultural importations.

On the whole, concerns about homogenization seemed overblown, and there were some specific cases in point. To be sure, Westernization has meant that most societies, including the West, have urban downtowns that look fairly similar and that they share many consumer products and outlets and also styles of dress and grooming. Most now have rough commonalities in aspects of educational structure and commitments to some scientific training and capacities to contribute to scientific research, now clearly a global enterprise. Many share the broad outlines of parliamentary democracy, with India and Japan, for example, fully as successful and durable as democratic states as several key Western entries. Quite a few, finally, participate in modern, or "international" art styles. Correspondingly it is less easy to identify the West by its marked contrast with, say, South Korea than it was a hundred years ago, when Western contact with the peninsula was in its infancy.

But civilizational flavors are hardly lost. Japan, for example, has been globalizing and Westernizing, in many respects, for about a century and a half. Yet it is hardly Western. Its parliamentary democracy has a distinctive style, and its overlap between state and private enterprise is different from the West as well. Strong group consciousness contrasts with greater Western individualism. When Japan borrowed the quiz show entertainment form from the United States it added elaborate shaming for contestants who failed – perfectly logical in the culture, but hardly Western despite the shared game format. Gender distinctions, also, are different from, and on the whole greater, than in the West. None of this means that Japan is inferior, or that

Japan and the West are on some collision course. But the Japanese example shows clearly that the most probable results of extensive borrowing from the West involves a combination of overlap, distinctive amalgamations of tradition and Western form (as with the quiz shows), and some traditional elements outright. And this means, in turn, that a number of Western characteristics, like individualism, can still be defined against a Japanese comparative backdrop.

Given globalization, members of elites in many societies move easily in and out of the West; some call themselves, appropriately enough, "bicultural." They visit the United States and Western Europe often and frequently have relatives who live there permanently. They keep contact with Western pop culture, and sometimes their education has maintained more traditional Western elements than Western education itself now does. Educated Indians, for instance, may have read more Shakespeare than their English, certainly their American counterparts. But again, sharing need not produce identity. The same Indians who mix so readily and engagingly, speaking English more often than Hindi, are also likely to practice arranged marriage, which, despite its merits in promoting marital stability, is simply not consistent with current Western values.

Overlap may increase further with time. Defining the characteristics of Western civilization may require increasing subtlety, and the number of really distinctive features – a commitment to science, for example – may decline as other societies join in. But there is little imminent likelihood that Western civilization, with its characteristic advantages and drawbacks, will quickly be lost in a larger sea of global Westernization.

Western hesitancies

A final aspect requires comment. Despite their dominance of many aspects of globalization thus far, many Westerners are not entirely happy with the process. This includes those most directly affected, because of their environmental commitments or fears of job loss to low-wage areas. But the concerns spill over more widely.

Among Europeans, two issues loom large. The first involves the extent to which globalization seems to be Americanization, threatening European identity in the process. The stake here is cultural. Europeans have done fine, on the whole, in maintaining their share in the global economy, often buying American companies, like Holiday Inn or Burger King, in the process. But the battle for culture is tougher, because the United States, with its large market and its enthusiasm for mass consumerism, has long had the edge in this category. A French farmer gained international fame, and participation in anti-globalization protests, for his physical attack on a McDonald's outlet as being a threat to Frenchness. Again France: youth eating habits are troubling not only because of indulgence in fast foods but also because consumption of sugary sodas is going up 4.5% a year. And again the villain is the American model.

The second European concern, sharpening in the early 21st century, involves immigration, another clear concomitant of globalization. European nations, willing to reduce nationalism at the policy level, continue to define themselves in terms of considerable internal homogeneity. They have found it difficult to integrate growing numbers of immigrants, many of whom are revealingly called "guest workers." Few citizens from racial minorities are represented in elected legislatures or as major figures on television. A rise of right-wing sentiment in 2002 revealed a growing desire to limit non-Western immigration, despite the fact that, with rapidly ageing populations, the need for additional sources of labor may grow rather than contract.

A subset of this concern specifically involves Islam, the source of many of the immigrant streams to much of Western Europe. Long-standing fears of Islam, which go deep in the Western tradition, feed the more standard biases against immigrants as strange, unhygienic and potentially criminal. Globalization means increasing interaction between the West and Islam. Elements in Islam are clearly uncomfortable in the process, but the same applies to elements in the West as well. Globalization can force a confrontation with deep-seated components in a civilization's history.

For its part, the United States has remained more open to global immigrant streams, though the growing fears of terrorism have introduced some major new question marks. And, of course, Americanization is a non-issue. But globalization's potential to modify national sovereignty touches a sensitive nerve, the same nerve that vibrated to isolationism some decades before. Bolstered by its unusual military advantage, the United States in the first years of the 21st century pulled out of several international treaties, ranging from limits on the use of land mines to a pollution control agreement designed to limit global warming. Many Americans felt strongly that global collaborations must not limit their national freedom of action. As with European hesitancies, the American hesitations were revealing, particularly in a nation eager to urge cooperation and flexibility on others.

The West in the 21st century

Asked to highlight the qualities of their civilization at the outset of the 21st century, many Westerners would place tolerance high on their list, a quality honed from the Enlightenment onward. And in truth, despite some anxieties attached to globalization, many Westerners were open to the attributes of other cultures, from foods to art forms, adding them to their list of interests and enjoyments in a global age. With widespread imitation a sincere form of flattery, many Westerners could also feel comfortable with the validity of many of their characteristic institutions and values.

There were uncertainties for the future – as there always are. Not all the consequences of the relative decline in power position may yet have come home to roost. If combined with some of the new resentments of the West for its advantages in globalization, there could be significant challenges for the civilization in future. As noted earlier, one aspect of the nervous support for Western civ courses, in the current United States, was the hope that a white-washed past might provide comfort amid potential new problems to come.

Changes in age structure represented another interesting issue. Along with Japan, and thanks to pervasive birth rate limitation plus longevity advance, the West – particularly Western Europe – was rapidly acquiring another distinctive feature, in a far older population structure than any society had ever previously experienced, far older than the structure of most of the world's other civilizations as well. Only time would tell how this innovation would interact with other aspects of the society or affect its position in the world.

Younger than some of the world's successful civilization, Western civiliz-ation has nevertheless stood a test of considerable time. It has maintained some continuity with earlier iterations, including selective classical borrowings plus the more coherent identity launched with the Middle Ages. It has added some distinguishing features over the centuries, and dropped off a few. It survived a particularly demanding set of challenges during the first half of the 20th century, if not with grace at least with the possibility of renewal. It continues to play a significant world role, if with more selfishness and uncertainty than its leaders sometimes acknowledge. Its connections between past and present move on – again, as is true with the other great world civilizations – into the new century.

Further reading

Theodore von Laue, *The World Revolution of Westernization: The Twentieth Century in Global Perspective* (New York: Oxford University Press, 1987); Anthony Giddens, *Runaway World: How Globalization is Reshaping Our Lives* (New York: Routledge, 2000); Jan Aart Scholte, *Globalization: A Critical Introduction* (New York: St. Martin's Press, 2000); Paul Kirkbridge, ed., *Globalization, The External Pressures* (Chichester: Wiley, 2001).

Epilogue
Western civilization and Western civ

Western civilization has been a changing entity. The changes have included important new features, such as a heightened importance for science or the emergence of distinctive tensions between women and men. They have included some major failings, as in the addition of racism to a longer Western history of hostility to outsiders or the period in the early 20th century when the civilization nearly self-destructed. Amid change, including the more recent decades of revival, the civilization has retained a certain degree of coherence by building on key continuities from the Middle Ages and the selective revival of classical interests, and, of course, by retaining something of a core geography in western and central Europe.

This book has contended that, while often taught about, and often very well, Western civilization has been too rarely hauled out for examination as a civilization – and that this deficiency has needlessly complicated the relationship between Western civ and world history as subjects. Explicit analysis raises some new questions and produces new insights about familiar topics, for example the industrial revolution. It obviously tests the chronology of Western civilization, including the challenging issue of origins. It calls for more careful treatment of the relationships between the West and other parts of the world, in virtually every time period. And, at the end, it raises questions about the civilization's future in an age of globalization.

We have also noted the rise of a teaching tradition and a public commitment, focused on Western civ as the bearer of certain identities and values in a time of change and challenge. The attachments to Western civ may not adequately convey the richness of the subject, for they tend toward a narrow and celebratory approach. History helps us to understand how the world around us has emerged only if we deal with problems as well as triumphs and weaknesses along with strengths. Treating Western civ as a hallowed museum piece does not serve these purposes, and it does not in fact do justice to the dynamism of the subject.

The summons for Western civ – and all the civs – in the early 21st century involves reexamining relationships with the wider world. Globalization offers opportunities for new learning and new exposures. But it also offers challenges. In the case of the West, the challenges include both a set of traditions and a number of past behaviors that need to be modified at a time of changing power balances. They include key questions about the capacity of the West to adjust to new partners and competitors after an age of less complicated hegemony – an area on which recent evidence is, not surprisingly, somewhat mixed. Recognizing memories that other societies have about Western actions, and also acknowledging ways in which other traditions have helped shape the Western experience, must be part of this process. Many societies will work to combine a clear sense of identity with new global relationships; many will work at the difficult task of self-definition without distinctive or belligerent claims of superiority; Western civilization will surely be among them, or at least we can hope that it will be. But Western civ as a narrowly conservative mantra, clinging to memories of real or imagined past glories and resisting new insights and critiques, will not get the job done.

In terms of the American teaching tradition, this means in turn that a world history context for Western civ becomes absolutely imperative. We need active comparisons, a sense of how global forces and contacts have shaped the West, rather than the West in isolated glory or seen as an independent agent in world affairs. The challenge, in terms of new curricula and new teaching combinations, is exciting.

Index